Navigating An Insane World Filled With Bots

L.W. Sr. and L.W. Jr.

Copyright © 2024 by Authors

All rights reserved. No part of this publication may be reproduced in any form or by any means, electronic or mechanical, including photocopying, recording, or any information browsing, storage, or retrieval system, without permission in writing from the publisher.

Published in the United States
First Edition, 2024

Unless otherwise indicated, all the characters in this book are fictitious. Any resemblance to actual persons, living or dead, is purely coincidental.

Table of Content

Introduction 4

Chapter 1 13

Chapter 2 23

Chapter 3 34

Chapter 4 45

Chapter 5 57

Chapter 7 81

Chapter 8 94

Chapter 9 107

Chapter 10 119

Introduction

In the modern world, most people follow a set script that society provides. These individuals, whom we call bots, conform to societal norms, accept misinformation without question, and defend public figures or institutions with genuine emotional attachments. This book introduces bots as programmed members of society who rarely engage in deep critical thought, preferring to remain within the safety of their familiar beliefs.

The Nature of Bots

Bots are not inherently evil or malicious. Instead, they are products of a system designed to keep people within specific social, cultural, and intellectual boundaries. From an early age, media, education systems, and social expectations have conditioned bots to follow rules and avoid questioning the status quo. These influences shape Their emotional responses, making them loyal defenders of the prevailing societal narratives, even when these narratives may not serve their best interests.

Bots find comfort in structure and authority. They rely on external validation from peers, celebrities, or institutions to form their opinions. This reliance creates a reinforcement cycle where new information that challenges their worldview is either ignored or fiercely rejected. The media plays a significant role in this process, often promoting emotionally charged content that keeps bots in constant engagement but minimal reflection.

This behavior is perplexing and frustrating for non-bots, those who see beyond the veil of societal programming. How can so many people believe things that are so clearly false or harmful? The key lies in understanding the mechanisms that drive bots' behavior.

The Divide Between Bots and Non-Bots

This book's heart lies the central theme: the divide between bots and non-bots. Non-bots challenge societal norms, think critically about the information they receive, and refuse to accept surface-level truths. While bots find comfort in conformity, non-bots thrive on questioning and exploring ideas that challenge the status quo.

This divide creates a natural tension between bots and non-bots, especially in social and familial interactions. For example, non-bots may be seen as troublemakers or contrarians because they challenge widely accepted beliefs or question the motivations of public figures. Meanwhile, bots may view non-bots as unnecessarily combative, complex, or even conspiratorial, especially when non-bots present facts or evidence that undermine their emotionally held beliefs.

This divide is evident in everyday situations:

Social Media Echo Chambers: Bots thrive in environments that reflect their existing beliefs. Algorithms on platforms like Facebook or Twitter reinforce their worldview by presenting content that aligns with their emotions and perspectives, deepening their conformity.

Workplace Conversations: In professional settings, non-bots may find it challenging to engage in meaningful dialogue when their colleagues are more concerned with fitting in than challenging ideas. The pressure to conform to corporate culture or avoid challenging superiors' opinions leads to the suppression of independent thought.

Family Gatherings: Holidays and family events often highlight the divide between bots and non-bots, where discussions about politics, news, or social issues become emotionally defensible. Non-bots struggle to engage in rational conversations, as bots cling to emotionally charged narratives reinforced by the media.

For non-bots, the challenge is not just about thinking critically; it's about maintaining relationships and navigating social spaces where bot behavior dominates.

Navigating Societal Chaos, Misinformation, and Emotional Manipulation

The world we live in is increasingly chaotic, fueled by misinformation and emotional manipulation. Bots seek comfort in simplistic narratives and are especially vulnerable to these tactics. Governments, corporations, and media outlets have perfected the art of emotional manipulation, using fear, outrage, and tribalism to keep bots engaged. In this environment, non-bots must develop different skills to navigate the storm of falsehoods and emotional noise.

Non-bots see through the manipulation, but that doesn't make the experience less exhausting. From sensationalized headlines to viral social media posts, the modern world is filled with content designed to provoke strong emotional reactions rather than encourage deep thought. Bots, conditioned by a lifetime of emotional responses to stimuli, are quick to share and defend these emotionally charged stories, further spreading misinformation.

Consider the media coverage of a divisive political issue. Bots will often latch onto the first piece of information they receive, especially if it aligns with their preexisting beliefs. They'll share this information with their peers, who reinforce the narrative, creating a feedback loop of emotional validation. Even when confronted with contradictory facts, bots will often double down on their beliefs, unwilling to experience the discomfort of cognitive dissonance.

For non-bots, this creates a frustrating dynamic. How do you reason with someone emotionally invested in a false narrative? The key is not to confront bots head-on, as this often leads to defensiveness and emotional outbursts. Instead, non-bots must learn to blend in, carefully navigating conversations and social situations without provoking unnecessary conflict.

Blending In: The Non-Bot's Survival Strategy

In a world dominated by bots, non-bots often find themselves at odds with the majority. While the natural inclination of many non-bots is to challenge falsehoods directly, this approach usually leads to conflict, isolation, or burnout. Instead, this book advocates for a more subtle approach—blending in.

Blending in doesn't mean abandoning your principles or pretending to be something you're not. Instead, it's about understanding the dynamics at play and navigating social environments without paying unnecessary attention to your non-conformity. By mastering the art of blending in, non-bots can protect their mental and emotional well-being while still pursuing truth and authenticity.

Critical strategies for blending in include:

Listening More, Speaking Less: Non-bots can gather valuable information by listening carefully to what bots say and how they react. This allows non-bots to assess the situation before deciding whether to engage or disengage.

Mirroring: A subtle form of social adaptation, mirroring involves reflecting the tone, body language, or even speech patterns of bots to make interactions smoother and less aggressive.

Picking Your Battles: Not every conversation is worth having. Non-bots must learn when to push for deeper dialogue and when to step back, preserving their energy for moments when their input will truly matter.

The Emotional Toll of Being a Non-Bot

Living in a bot-dominated world can take an emotional toll on non-bots. The constant exposure to misinformation, the frustration of reasoning with emotionally driven bots, and isolation from mainstream society can lead to emotional exhaustion. Non-bots must be mindful of their mental health and practice self-care strategies to avoid burnout.

This book will offer practical advice for non-bots on how to protect their mental well-being. From mindfulness exercises to strategies for disengaging from toxic environments, non-bots will learn how to stay grounded while navigating the chaos of a bot-filled world.

Conclusion

This book aims to help non-bots understand the dynamics of a bot-dominated world and develop the skills necessary to navigate it successfully. By learning how to recognize bot behavior, blend in, and protect their mental health, non-bots can survive—and even thrive—in a world that often feels insane. This book is a guide to surviving the chaos and maintaining your truth and authenticity in a world that resists both.

Chapter 1

Understanding The Bot

The world is filled with individuals who seem content to live in a state of unawareness, accepting surface-level truths and societal narratives without question. These people, called bots, are not inherently malicious or intentionally ignorant. Still, they often choose ignorance because it feels safer and more comfortable than confronting the world's complexities. This chapter will dive into the psychological and sociological reasons why people remain unaware, the mechanisms that drive their decision to ignore inconvenient truths, and how this plays out in real-life scenarios involving family, friends, and workplace environments.

Psychological Factors: Fear of Discomfort and Cognitive Dissonance

One of the primary reasons people remain unaware is the psychological discomfort that comes with questioning deeply held beliefs or challenging long-standing societal norms. This discomfort manifests in various ways, often leading individuals to choose ignorance over complex critical thinking tasks. Two major psychological factors contribute to this phenomenon: fear of pain and cognitive dissonance.

Fear of Discomfort

Humans are creatures of habit, and one of our deepest instincts is to avoid physical or mental discomfort. The idea that one's long-held beliefs could be incorrect or that society's trusted institutions could be misleading is an uncomfortable thought. Rather than confront this, most people prefer to retreat into the safety of ignorance, where everything feels predictable and reassuring.

Mental and Emotional Safety: For bots, ignorance offers psychological safety. When confronted with conflicting information or evidence that contradicts their worldview, bots instinctively protect themselves by rejecting the new information. Accepting that they've been misled or their beliefs might be wrong can feel like a personal attack, as their identity is often intertwined with these beliefs.

Avoiding Uncertainty: Uncertainty is deeply unsettling for most people. The unknown creates anxiety, and many bots would rather cling to familiar, albeit false, narratives than venture into the uncertain territory of seeking truth. Ignorance provides a false sense of stability, even though this stability comes at the cost of intellectual growth.

Cognitive Dissonance

Another critical psychological mechanism is cognitive dissonance, when individuals experience discomfort from holding two contradictory beliefs or when new information conflicts with their worldview. Bots often experience cognitive dissonance when confronted with facts or perspectives that challenge their preconceived notions.

Avoiding Dissonance: Bots often dismiss or rationalize conflicting information to avoid the mental strain of reconciling contradictory beliefs. Rather than adapting their worldview to incorporate new truths, they either ignore the evidence or explain it away as an anomaly.

Emotional Reactions: Cognitive dissonance can trigger strong emotional reactions in bots, including anger, frustration, and defensiveness. When their beliefs are challenged, bots often respond with emotional outbursts to protect themselves from the discomfort of reevaluating their position. This emotional defensiveness further entrenches their unawareness and makes meaningful dialogue difficult. Example: A bot who strongly identifies with a particular political party may experience cognitive dissonance when presented with evidence that contradicts their party's platform. Rather than reconsider their political allegiance, they may dismiss the evidence as biased or accuse the person delivering the information of having ulterior motives. In doing so, they protect their identity and avoid the discomfort of questioning their worldview.

Case Studies: How Bots Respond in Real-Life Family and Workplace Scenarios

To better understand how these psychological factors manifest in everyday life, we will examine case studies illustrating how bots respond to challenges or confrontations with uncomfortable truths in family and workplace settings. These real-life examples will highlight how bots retreat into ignorance when faced with new information that challenges their beliefs.

Case Study 1: Family Dynamics at Holiday Gatherings

Family gatherings often serve as the perfect environment for bots to defend their unawareness. Consider the case of a family holiday dinner where a discussion about climate change emerges. A non-bot cousin raises scientific evidence about rising sea levels and greenhouse gases. The bot family members, who have long believed that climate change is a hoax, quickly shut down the conversation by citing vague counterarguments they've heard from biased news sources.

Emotional Defensiveness: Rather than engaging with the facts, the bot family members feel personally attacked. Their response isn't grounded in logic but in emotional defense mechanisms. The conversation becomes charged with emotional energy, making it impossible for the non-bot to introduce rational discourse.

Reinforcing Group Beliefs: In this scenario, the bots often seek support from other family members who share their views, creating a group dynamic where ignorance is reinforced. This groupthink mentality allows them to feel validated in their beliefs, even if those beliefs are misinformed.

Case Study 2: Workplace Conformity

Challenging the status quo or introducing new ideas can be risky in professional environments, especially in bots-dominated workplaces. Consider the example of a non-bot employee in a corporate office who suggests implementing a more sustainable business practice. The proposal is rejected by colleagues who dismiss it as unnecessary or too difficult to implement, citing outdated practices as their justification.

Avoiding Change: Bots in the workplace often fear change because it threatens the familiar systems they've grown comfortable with. Even when the non-bot presents clear evidence of the benefits of sustainability, the bots remain unconvinced because accepting the proposal would require them to rethink their work processes and potentially disrupt the status quo.

Peer Pressure: In bot-dominated workplaces, peer pressure plays a significant role in maintaining unawareness. Employees who resist change often band together to discourage the non-bot from pushing for reforms, using phrases like, "That's just how things are done here" or "We've always done it this way."

Example: A non-bot employee working in marketing suggests using data analytics to optimize ad campaigns, but their bot colleagues resist the idea, preferring to rely on outdated marketing strategies. Rather than engaging with the evidence, the bots claim that analytics is "just a trend" and dismiss the idea altogether, avoiding the discomfort of learning a new system.

The Comfort Zone of Ignorance: Why Ignorance Feels Safer Than the Truth

At its core, unawareness is often a deliberate choice. While some may remain ignorant due to a lack of exposure to certain information, many bots choose ignorance because it offers a protective comfort zone. In this context, ignorance is not simply a lack of knowledge but an intentional retreat from the truth.

Emotional Comfort and Security

Bots seek emotional comfort in familiar narratives, even if those narratives are inaccurate or incomplete. The emotional safety of ignorance protects bots from the anxiety of facing the unknown or having to confront brutal realities.

Stability vs. Truth: Ignorance provides a sense of stability that truth often disrupts. For many bots, stability is more valuable than intellectual growth or self-awareness, leading them to avoid information that could threaten their mental equilibrium actively.

Cognitive Ease: Ignorance is easier than truth-seeking. Engaging with complex issues requires mental effort, critical thinking, and a willingness to adapt. For bots, it's far more comfortable to remain in cognitive ease, accepting simple, emotionally satisfying answers to complex questions.

The Threat of Isolation

Non-bots who challenge the mainstream narrative often face isolation, and bots, fearing this same fate, choose to conform rather than question. The idea of being ostracized by one's social group or family can be terrifying for bots, leading them to cling to group beliefs rather than risking isolation by questioning the consensus.

Social Belonging: For bots, maintaining their ignorance is often tied to keeping their social connections. They fear that questioning the group's beliefs will lead to rejection, so they suppress any doubts or concerns to maintain harmony.

Example: In a group of friends who all share the same political beliefs, a bot may suppress their doubts about specific policies to avoid being seen as disloyal to the group. The fear of losing their social standing outweighs the desire to seek truth.

Conclusion

Understanding the psychological and sociological reasons behind unawareness is critical to navigating a bot-dominated world. By recognizing the role of fear of discomfort, cognitive dissonance, and the comfort zone of ignorance, non-bots can better understand why many people remain unaware, even in the face of overwhelming evidence. This understanding is essential for non-bots as they learn to navigate interactions with bots, recognizing when it is worth engaging and when it is best to let go.

Chapter 2

Recognizing Different Types of Unawareness

Ignorance manifests in many forms, and it's essential to understand the varying degrees of unawareness that exist in society. Not all ignorance is created equal; some result from a genuine lack of access to information, while others are deeply rooted in willful avoidance of the truth. This chapter will break down the different types of ignorance, ranging from minor misconceptions to deliberate, willful ignorance. By understanding these distinctions, non-bots can better navigate interactions with bots, recognizing when education or dialogue may be effective and when engagement is futile.

Unintentional vs. Willful Ignorance

The first and most important distinction when understanding ignorance is whether it is unintentional or willful. These two categories define how bots interact with the world and react when presented with new information.

Unintentional Ignorance

Unintentional ignorance occurs when individuals are simply unaware of certain information, not because they are actively avoiding it but because they haven't been exposed to it or haven't had the opportunity to learn about it. In a world saturated with information, no one can know everything and unintentional ignorance is a common and understandable part of human life.

Lack of Exposure: Many bots haven't been exposed to specific ideas or facts. For instance, someone may be unaware of the specifics of climate change or the historical context of political conflicts because they haven't encountered these topics in their education or daily life.

Misinformation: In some cases, bots are unintentionally ignorant because they have been fed misinformation. The media, political institutions, or social networks may have provided them with incomplete or false information they believe to be true. In this case, their ignorance is not malicious; they are victims of misinformation.

Genuine Misconceptions: Unintentional ignorance often stems from misunderstandings or incomplete knowledge. Bots may hold beliefs based on outdated or simplified versions of reality, which can be corrected with the right information.

Example: A bot who grew up in a community with limited access to education might have unintentional ignorance about scientific topics. They may not understand complex concepts like evolution or quantum physics simply because they haven't had the opportunity to learn about them.

Willful Ignorance

Willful ignorance, on the other hand, occurs when individuals deliberately avoid or reject information that contradicts their existing beliefs or worldview. These bots remain ignorant because the truth is too uncomfortable, challenging, or threatening to their sense of identity.

Refusal to Engage: Willfully ignorant bots actively avoid engaging with new information. They may refuse to read articles, watch documentaries, or participate in discussions that could challenge their beliefs. This is often done to preserve their emotional comfort or avoid the cognitive dissonance from confronting new truths.

Selective Information Consumption: Willfully ignorant bots often consume media or information that reinforces their worldview while avoiding sources that present alternative perspectives. This selective engagement allows them to maintain their ignorance while feeling as though they are informed.

Emotional Defense Mechanism: For many willfully ignorant bots, ignorance is a defense mechanism. Accepting new information would force them to reconsider their identity, values, or social standing, so they ignore or dismiss anything that could disrupt their worldview.

Example: A bot who refuses to acknowledge climate change despite overwhelming scientific evidence may do so because accepting the reality of climate change would force them to confront uncomfortable truths about their lifestyle, political beliefs, or economic interests.

Levels of Ignorance and Their Societal Impact

Ignorance exists on a spectrum, from minor misunderstandings to deeply entrenched, willful ignorance. Each level of ignorance has different consequences, both for the individual and for society as a whole. Understanding these levels can help non-bots navigate interactions with bots and assess the potential impact of ignorance on social dynamics.

Level 1: Minor Misconceptions

At the lowest level, ignorance takes the form of minor misconceptions—small errors in understanding that can often be easily corrected with a conversation or a quick fact-check. These misconceptions are typically not profoundly held and don't carry significant emotional weight, making it easier for non-bots to engage with bots and offer new information.

Examples: A person might believe a common myth (e.g., that humans only use 10% of their brains) but readily accept the correction when presented with evidence.

Societal Impact: Minor misconceptions generally have limited societal impact. These types of ignorance are often harmless and can be corrected through education or simple dialogue. However, if left unchallenged, they can contribute to the broader culture of misinformation.

Level 2: Deeply Rooted Misinformation

At the next level, ignorance becomes more entrenched, often because it is reinforced by misinformation from trusted sources. Bots at this level have been exposed to incorrect information and have internalized it as fact, making it harder to change their minds. This ignorance is more dangerous because it is often tied to influential narratives spread by media, political groups, or social networks.

Examples: A person may believe that vaccines cause autism, a myth perpetuated by discredited studies and misinformation campaigns. This belief may be reinforced by social media networks or political figures, making it harder to challenge.

Societal Impact: Deeply rooted misinformation has a significant impact on society. It can influence public health decisions, voting patterns, and social behaviors, creating widespread consequences. Non-bots who attempt to correct this ignorance often face resistance, as bots may feel emotionally invested in the misinformation.

Level 3: Willful Ignorance

At the highest level, willful ignorance is deeply entrenched and emotionally charged. Bots who choose willful ignorance are misinformed and actively resistant to learning new information. They may reject evidence, avoid discussions, or attack those who challenge their beliefs. This ignorance is hazardous because it is driven by emotional investment rather than a lack of information.

Examples: A bot who denies the existence of systemic racism despite overwhelming evidence may do so because acknowledging it would challenge their worldview and identity. This bot is unlikely to change their perspective, even with clear facts or personal stories contradicting their beliefs.

Societal Impact: Willful ignorance has the most destructive societal impact. It fuels division, perpetuates harmful ideologies, and prevents meaningful dialogue. Bots who engage in willful ignorance contribute to polarization, making it difficult for non-bots to create positive change.

The Emotional Investment Bots Have In Maintaining Ignorance

One of the most critical factors that sustain ignorance, especially willful ignorance, is bots' emotional investment in their beliefs. Many bots' beliefs are tied to their identity, social standing, or sense of security. Challenging these beliefs would require them to confront uncomfortable truths and risk alienating them from their social circles or forcing them to rethink their place in the world.

Emotional Attachment To Beliefs

Many bots are emotionally attached to their beliefs, which makes it difficult for them to engage with new information. Several factors can drive this attachment:

Identity: Bots may see their beliefs as part of their core identity. For example, a bot identifying strongly with a particular political ideology may reject any information that contradicts it because it feels like a personal attack.

Social Connections: Bots may maintain their ignorance to preserve social connections. In many cases, people adopt the beliefs of their social group to avoid conflict or rejection. Challenging those beliefs could lead to social isolation, a powerful motivator for remaining ignorant.

Emotional Comfort: Ignorance often provides emotional comfort by protecting bots from the discomfort of cognitive dissonance. For example, a bot who believes in conspiracy theories may find emotional satisfaction in feeling like they have special knowledge that others lack, even if that knowledge is false.

Cognitive Dissonance and Emotional Defensiveness

When bots are confronted with information that challenges their beliefs, they often experience cognitive dissonance, a psychological tension that arises from holding two contradictory ideas. To resolve this discomfort, bots defend their beliefs rather than engage with the new information. This emotional defensiveness can take several forms:

Anger: Bots may respond with anger when their beliefs are challenged, which helps them protect their emotional investment in those beliefs.

Denial: In many cases, bots will deny the validity of the new information, choosing instead to retreat into the comfort of their existing worldview.

Rationalization: Bots may attempt to rationalize the new information in a way that allows them to maintain their original beliefs. For example, they may dismiss contradictory evidence as biased or claim that the latest information is part of a larger conspiracy.

Conclusion

Ignorance exists on a spectrum, from minor misconceptions to deeply entrenched, willful ignorance. By understanding the different levels of ignorance and the emotional factors that sustain it, non-bots can better navigate their interactions with bots. Recognizing when ignorance is unintentional and willful allows non-bots to approach these interactions strategically, knowing when education may be effective and when it is best to disengage. The next chapter will explore how non-bots can adapt and blend into a bot-dominated world without sacrificing authenticity.

Chapter 3

The Importance Of Blending In

In a world where bots dominate social, familial, and professional environments, non-bots must navigate carefully to avoid conflict and maintain harmonious relationships. While non-bots often value authenticity and truth-seeking, openly challenging the status quo can lead to social isolation, emotional strain, and unnecessary conflict. This chapter explores why non-bots must blend in with bots, their strategies to balance adaptation and authenticity, and real-life examples of non-bots successfully integrating into bot-dominated spaces without sacrificing their values.

The Necessity of Avoiding Direct Confrontation

Many non-bots are inclined to challenge false narratives directly or call out uncritical thinking when encountering them. However, this approach can backfire in many cases, leading to strained relationships, heated arguments, or even social exclusion. The key to navigating a world filled with bots lies in understanding the delicate balance between sharing your perspective and maintaining peace.

Why Confrontation Doesn't Work

As discussed in earlier chapters, bots are often emotionally invested in their beliefs and opinions. When these beliefs are challenged, bots react defensively, emotionally, and sometimes aggressively. This defensive posture is rooted in their desire to avoid cognitive dissonance—the mental discomfort caused by holding contradictory beliefs.

Emotional Defensiveness: Bots are often highly emotional when their worldview is challenged, and confrontation can trigger anger, resentment, or hostility. When a bot's sense of identity is tied to their beliefs, they perceive challenges as personal attacks, leading to unproductive and emotionally charged interactions.

Escalating Conflict: In many cases, confrontation escalates into conflict, with neither party willing to listen or engage meaningfully. Non-bots may become frustrated by the bot's unwillingness to engage in rational dialogue, while bots may become increasingly defensive, further entrenching themselves in their beliefs.

Example: A non-bot who tries to argue with a family member at a holiday gathering about a political issue may find that the conversation quickly turns into an emotional battle, with the family member feeling attacked and the non-bot feeling unheard. What was intended as a rational discussion ends as a source of tension that may damage the relationship.

Social Harmony and Emotional Energy

By avoiding confrontation, non-bots can maintain social harmony and preserve emotional energy. Constantly engaging in debates or trying to change others' minds can be emotionally exhausting and, more often than not, fruitless. Non-bots must assess the social context before deciding whether to engage or step back.

Pick Your Battles: Non-bots need to learn when to engage and when to let things slide. Not every conversation needs to be a confrontation, and not every bot's belief needs to be corrected. In many cases, silence or neutrality may be the best way to preserve social relationships without sacrificing one's values.

Protecting Your Emotional Well-Being: Confrontation often leads to stress, frustration, and emotional exhaustion, especially when the non-bot is constantly bombarded with bot behavior. By disengaging from unproductive arguments, non-bots can protect their mental health and avoid the emotional toll of constant conflict.

Strategies for Balancing Authenticity and Adaptation

Blending in with bots doesn't mean abandoning authenticity or compromising core values. Instead, it involves developing strategies that allow non-bots to maintain their integrity while avoiding unnecessary conflict. Blending in is an art that requires subtlety, emotional intelligence, and strategic thinking.

Listening and Observing

One of the most potent strategies for blending in is to listen more and speak less. By carefully observing bots' behaviors, beliefs, and emotional responses, non-bots can gather valuable information about when and how to engage without triggering confrontation.

Gaining Insight into Bot Behavior: Non-bots can use active listening to understand the emotional drivers behind a bot's beliefs. What are the bots most passionate about? What triggers their defensiveness? By understanding these cues, non-bots can avoid stepping into conversational minefields.

Building Rapport: Listening is also a tool for building rapport and trust. Bots are likelier to engage in meaningful dialogue when they feel heard and understood. By practicing empathy and showing genuine interest in the bot's perspective, non-bots can lay the groundwork for more productive future conversations.

Example: A non-bot who listens to a coworker's rant about conspiracy theories at the office without immediately countering their points can better understand the coworker's emotional investment in these beliefs. By observing rather than confronting, the non-bot maintains peace in the workplace while learning when it might be appropriate to introduce alternative perspectives.

Mirroring and Adaptation

Another effective strategy is mirroring, a technique in which non-bots subtly reflect bots' body language, tone, or conversational style to build rapport and avoid conflict. This doesn't mean abandoning one's beliefs but adapting one's communication style to fit the context.

Mirroring Speech Patterns: Non-bots can adopt similar speech patterns, using language that aligns with the bot's communication style. For example, if bots tend to use emotional language, non-bots can mirror this by acknowledging their emotions without agreeing with their conclusions.

Body Language and Tone: Non-bots can also use body language and tone to de-escalate potentially confrontational situations. Maintaining a calm, open posture and a neutral or compassionate tone can help diffuse tension and keep conversations civil.

Example: A non-bot in a politically charged conversation might use phrases like, "I see where you're coming from" or "That's an interesting point" to acknowledge the bot's perspective without endorsing it. By mirroring the bot's tone and language, the non-bot keeps the conversation calm and non-confrontational, preserving the relationship while maintaining their views.

Choosing Neutral Topics

In situations where confrontation is likely, non-bots can avoid conflict by steering conversations toward neutral or less emotionally charged topics. This allows for social interaction without the risk of triggering defensiveness or hostility.

Redirection: If a conversation begins to head into controversial territory, non-bots can gently redirect it to safer subjects, such as shared hobbies, current events without emotional stakes, or general topics that don't touch on deeply held beliefs.

Finding Common Ground: Non-bots can also focus on finding common ground with bots. While non-bots may disagree with a bot's worldview, there are often shared values or interests that can serve as a foundation for peaceful interaction.

Example: If a family dinner conversation turns toward a divisive political issue, a non-bot might steer the conversation toward a less charged topic, such as travel plans, a favorite movie, or a neutral family story. This strategy keeps the social interaction pleasant without compromising the non-bot's values.

Real-Life Examples of Non-Bots Successfully Blending In Without Compromising Values

To illustrate how non-bots can blend in without sacrificing their authenticity, let's explore several real-life examples of non-bots successfully navigating difficult social, familial, and professional situations.

Example 1: The Thanksgiving Debate

A non-bot finds themselves at a family Thanksgiving dinner where a relative starts spouting politically charged misinformation. Rather than directly confronting the relative, the non-bot listens patiently, nodding occasionally to show they're engaged without agreeing with the statements being made. When asked for their opinion, the non-bot deflects by saying, "I haven't done enough research on that topic to comment," effectively disengaging from the debate without causing conflict.

Outcome: The non-bot successfully avoids arguments and maintains peace at the family gathering. The relative feels heard, but the non-bot doesn't have to compromise their values by engaging in misinformation or emotional debate.

Example 2: Navigating Workplace Politics

A non-bot works in an office where most colleagues subscribe to a particular political ideology. During lunch breaks, the conversation often turns toward political topics that the non-bot disagrees with. Rather than openly expressing their differing views, the non-bot listens, nods, and occasionally asks neutral questions to keep the conversation going. When pressed for their opinion, the non-bot responds, "I'm still thinking it through," and changes the subject to a work-related topic.

Outcome: The non-bot avoids alienating themselves from their colleagues, maintains professional relationships, and preserves their emotional energy for more important matters.

Example 3: Maintaining Friendships Despite Differing Beliefs

A non-bot has a close friend who frequently shares conspiracy theories on social media. Rather than confronting the friend about these beliefs, the non-bot focuses their conversations on shared interests, such as movies, books, or hobbies. When the friend brings up conspiracy theories in conversation, the non-bot acknowledges the friend's perspective without agreeing, then gently redirects the conversation toward a more neutral topic.

Outcome: The non-bot can maintain the friendship without endorsing the friend's conspiracy beliefs. The relationship remains intact, and the non-bot preserves their authenticity by avoiding unnecessary confrontation.

Conclusion

Blending in doesn't mean abandoning your values or compromising your integrity. Instead, it's about strategically navigating a world filled with bots by choosing when to engage, when to listen, and when to remain neutral. By avoiding confrontation, using strategies like mirroring and adaptation, and finding neutral topics for conversation, non-bots can maintain social harmony without losing themselves in the process.

Chapter 4

Techniques for Blending In

To navigate a world dominated by bots without being drawn into conflict or feeling isolated, non-bots must develop practical strategies to blend into bot-dominated environments while maintaining their non-bot mindset. This chapter provides actionable techniques to help non-bots integrate seamlessly into conversations, social circles, and workplaces. Through active listening, mirroring, and mastering diplomatic language, non-bots can minimize provocation, maintain relationships, and avoid unnecessary conflicts.

Active Listening and Speaking Less

Listening is an art, especially in a world where bots dominate conversations with emotionally charged narratives. One of the most essential strategies for non-bots to master is active listening, which involves paying close attention to what bots say without feeling the need to counter or correct their viewpoints immediately. Active listening allows non-bots to maintain social harmony, avoid conflict, and gather valuable insights into the mindset of bots.

The Value of Listening

Bots often seek validation through their conversations. They want to feel heard and understood; when they do, they are less likely to become defensive. By listening more than they speak, non-bots can diffuse tension before it arises.

Listening as a De-escalation Tool: Active listening helps de-escalate potentially confrontational situations. By allowing bots to express their opinions without interruption, non-bots create a space where bots feel validated and less likely to push for confrontation.

Avoiding the Need to Correct: One of the challenges non-bots face is the temptation to correct or counter every piece of misinformation. Active listening encourages non-bots to focus on understanding rather than fixing. This reduces conflict and allows for more harmonious interactions.

Example: A non-bot attends a family gathering where the conversation turns to a controversial social issue. Rather than jumping in to offer a differing opinion, the non-bot listens attentively, asking neutral questions like, "Can you tell me more about how you came to that conclusion?" This allows the bots in the conversation to feel heard while the non-bot avoids escalating the discussion.

The Power of Silence

Silence can be an effective tool for non-bots who want to avoid confrontation while participating in social interactions. By speaking less, non-bots can minimize the chances of triggering emotional responses from bots.

Letting Bots Speak Themselves Out: Often, bots will continue talking until they have fully expressed their emotional investment in a topic. By remaining silent, non-bots allow bots to exhaust their points without engaging in debate, thus avoiding unnecessary conflict.

Strategic Silence: Non-bots can also use strategic silence to create reflection space or subtly steer the conversation away from charged topics. When a bot finishes speaking, pausing or being silent can signal that the non-bot is considering what has been said without necessarily agreeing.

Example: At a work meeting, a non-bot listens silently as a colleague presents an idea based on misinformation. Instead of jumping in to correct them, the non-bot remains silent, allowing the conversation to continue without conflict. The silence gives the non-bot time to assess the situation and decide whether it's worth engaging or to remain neutral.

How to Ask Neutral Questions

Asking questions is a powerful way to engage without provoking defensiveness. When used correctly, questions can help bots feel validated while subtly introducing doubt or encouraging them to think more critically about their views.

Clarifying Questions: Non-bots can ask clarifying questions to keep the conversation going without appearing aggressive. For example, asking, "What makes you feel that way?" or "What led you to that conclusion?" allows bots to explain their reasoning without feeling attacked.

Reflective Questions: Reflective questions encourage bots to think more deeply about their views without directly challenging them. Phrases like, "Have you considered other perspectives on that?" or "What do you think about the research on this topic?" can guide bots toward considering alternative viewpoints without feeling pressured.

Example: A non-bot in a social circle hears a bot express a common misconception about a scientific topic. Rather than correcting them outright, the non-bot asks, "That's interesting—what sources did you find that information from?" This question prompts the bot to think about the validity of their sources, subtly encouraging them to reconsider their beliefs.

Mirroring Body Language and Speech Patterns

Non-bots can use mirroring to blend in more effectively in bot-dominated environments. Mirroring involves subtly imitating bots' body language, speech patterns, and conversational style to build rapport and reduce tension. Mirroring allows non-bots to fit in skillfully without compromising their core beliefs or values.

Mirroring Body Language

People are often more comfortable with others who exhibit similar body language. Non-bots can use this to their advantage by observing and subtly adopting bots' physical gestures, posture, and movements in social situations.

Posture and Gestures: Non-bots can mirror the posture and gestures of bots to create a sense of familiarity. For example, if a bot leans forward while speaking, the non-bot can do the same. If a bot uses open gestures like open palms or relaxed shoulders, the non-bot can mirror these cues to foster a sense of connection.

Subtle Adjustments: The key to successful mirroring is subtlety. Non-bots should avoid apparent mimicry, which can come across as disingenuous. Instead, they should focus on making minor adjustments that align with the bot's body language without entirely copying it.

Example: During a meeting, a non-bot observes that their colleague frequently crosses their arms while speaking. To build rapport, the non-bot subtly mirrors this gesture by crossing their arms, creating a subconscious connection between the two.

Mirroring Speech Patterns

Just as non-bots can mirror body language, they can also mirror speech patterns to build rapport. By reflecting the tone, pace, and style of a bot's speech, non-bots can blend into conversations more seamlessly.

Tone and Pace: If a bot speaks quickly and energetically, a non-bot can match this pace to create a sense of alignment. Conversely, if the bot speaks slowly and calmly, the non-bot can adjust its tone to reflect the same energy.

Vocabulary and Expressions: Non-bots can adopt similar vocabulary or expressions to foster a sense of common ground. For example, if a bot uses specific slang or catchphrases, the non-bot can subtly incorporate these into their speech to create a smoother interaction.

Example: A non-bot in a casual conversation notices that the bot they're speaking with uses a lot of humor and casual language. The non-bot mirrors this style by adopting a light-hearted tone and throwing in a few jokes, making the conversation feel more natural and aligned.

Diplomatic Language Skills to Avoid Provocation

Language is a powerful tool that non-bots can use to avoid provocation under challenging conversations. Diplomatic language involves using neutral, non-committal phrases that acknowledge the bot's perspective without endorsing or challenging it directly. This technique allows non-bots to participate in conversations without causing conflict, maintaining social harmony while preserving their integrity.

Using Neutral Phrasing

One of the most effective ways to avoid provoking bots is to use neutral phrasing that acknowledges their perspective without taking a firm stance. By choosing words carefully, non-bots can engage in conversations without becoming confrontational.

Non-Committal Language: Non-bots can use phrases like, "That's an interesting viewpoint" or "I can see why you'd think that" to acknowledge the bot's beliefs without agreeing or disagreeing. This keeps the conversation neutral and prevents the bot from feeling challenged.

Softening Statements: To avoid triggering defensiveness, non-bots can soften their statements by using qualifiers like "perhaps," "maybe," or "it seems." These words reduce the perceived certainty of the statement, making it less likely to provoke a strong emotional reaction from bots.

Example: A non-bot discussing a controversial topic with a bot at a family dinner might say, "That's an interesting perspective. I'm not sure I have all the information to form an opinion yet," effectively neutralizing the conversation without engaging in conflict.

Avoiding Absolutes

Bots often respond negatively to absolute statements, which can be rigid or confrontational. Non-bots can avoid provocation by steering clear of absolutes like "always," "never," or "everyone." Instead, they can use more flexible language that leaves room for interpretation.

Avoiding "Always" and "Never": Non-bots should avoid using language that implies certainty or generalization. Instead of saying, "That's always the case," a non-bot can say, "That seems to happen often," which softens the statement and makes it less aggressive.

Encouraging Openness: Non-bots can use open-ended statements to facilitate dialogue without taking a firm stance. Phrases like, "I'm curious to hear more about your view" or "I'd love to understand your perspective better" invite the bot to explain their position without feeling attacked.

Example: In a work discussion about a contentious issue, a non-bot avoids saying, "That idea never works." Instead, they say, "I've seen that

Conclusion: Summary of Chapter

In a bot-dominated world, blending in as a non-bot requires strategic communication, emotional intelligence, and subtle adaptation. This chapter outlined practical techniques that allow non-bots to maintain authenticity while avoiding conflict. Through active listening, non-bots can gather valuable insights without engaging in unnecessary debate. Mirroring body language and speech patterns helps non-bots build rapport and maintain harmony in social and professional environments. Finally, mastering diplomatic language skills ensures that non-bots can participate in conversations without triggering defensiveness or provoking confrontation.

These techniques are not about abandoning non-bot principles but adapting to a world where bots dominate conversations, narratives, and emotional exchanges. By learning when to speak, how to listen, and how to steer conversations diplomatically, non-bots can easily protect their mental and emotional well-being while navigating bot-dominated spaces. This chapter equips non-bots with the tools they need to blend in without compromising their integrity, allowing them to thrive in environments where critical thinking is often the exception.

Chapter 5

Navigating Family Dynamics as a Non-Bot

One of the most challenging environments for non-bots is their own family. Family dynamics are deeply emotional, and when family members are attached to societal narratives, challenging these beliefs can lead to tension, conflict, or estrangement. This chapter explores how non-bots can maintain meaningful relationships with family members who may be emotionally invested in mainstream narratives, providing strategies to avoid confrontation, set boundaries, and use empathy to maintain connections without sacrificing authenticity.

Avoiding Confrontation During Family Discussions

Family gatherings are often emotionally charged environments where long-standing beliefs and social norms are reinforced. When topics like politics, social issues, or personal values arise, non-bots may feel compelled to correct misinformation or challenge uncritical thinking. However, directly confronting family members on sensitive topics can lead to conflict and resentment, damaging family relationships.

Understanding Emotional Triggers

Family members, especially those who adhere to societal narratives, are often deeply emotionally invested in their beliefs. Challenging these beliefs can feel like a personal attack, leading to defensiveness, frustration, or anger. Non-bots need to be aware of these emotional triggers and understand that many family members are not ready or willing to question their worldview.

The Role of Identity: Many family members' beliefs are closely tied to their identity and sense of belonging. Challenging their worldview can threaten their identity, making them more likely to react emotionally rather than engage in rational discussion.

Emotional Reactions: Non-bots must be prepared for emotional responses when societal narratives are challenged. Family members may become defensive or hurt, even if the non-bot intends to share information or clarify facts. These emotional reactions can quickly escalate into conflict if not handled carefully.

Example: At a family dinner, a non-bot may hear a relative expressing strong opinions about a current political issue based on misinformation. Rather than immediately challenging the relative's views, the non-bot can remain silent, avoiding direct confrontation and preserving the peace at the gathering.

Strategies for Defusing Conflict

To avoid confrontation during family discussions, non-bots can employ several strategies to navigate conversations without creating tension or escalating the situation.

Redirection: When a family discussion turns toward a contentious topic, non-bots can gently steer the conversation toward a more neutral subject. By shifting the focus of the debate, non-bots can prevent the conversation from becoming too heated or emotional.

Deflecting: When asked directly for their opinion on a sensitive issue, non-bots can deflect by using phrases like, "I'm not sure I know enough about that topic" or "It's something I'm still thinking through." This deflection allows non-bots to avoid engaging without taking a firm stance that could provoke conflict.

Neutral Statements: Non-bots can offer neutral statements acknowledging the family member's perspective without endorsing or rejecting it. Phrases like, "That's an interesting viewpoint" or "I can see why you might feel that way" help de-escalate tension without fully engaging in the debate.

Example: A non-bot overhears a heated discussion about a divisive political issue at a family reunion. Instead of joining the debate, the non-bot gently redirects the conversation by asking about a recent family event or sharing a lighthearted story. Changing the subject helps the non-bot defuse the situation and prevent the conversation from escalating into an argument.

Setting Boundaries While Maintaining Harmony

Setting boundaries with family members is crucial for non-bots who want to protect their mental and emotional well-being. However, maintaining harmony while setting boundaries can be challenging, especially in close-knit families where specific topics or beliefs are deeply ingrained. Non-bots must balance preserving family relationships and asserting their need for personal space or respectful communication.

Communicating Boundaries

Establishing clear boundaries is essential for avoiding situations that lead to conflict or emotional distress. Non-bots should communicate their boundaries in a calm, respectful manner, making it clear that while they value their family relationships, they need certain limits to maintain their well-being.

Be Clear and Direct: When setting boundaries, non-bots should be clear and direct about what they are comfortable discussing and what topics they prefer to avoid. For example, a non-bot might say, "I would rather not discuss politics during family gatherings because it often leads to unnecessary arguments."

Use "I" Statements: To avoid sounding accusatory, non-bots can use "I" statements to express their boundaries. For example, "I feel uncomfortable when our conversations turn into debates, so I would appreciate it if we could focus on lighter topics during family dinners."

Firm, Yet Compassionate: Non-bots can assert their boundaries firmly while remaining compassionate. It's important to acknowledge the family member's feelings while standing firm in one's needs.

Example: A non-bot sets a boundary with a family member who frequently brings up controversial political topics at family gatherings. The non-bot calmly says, "I appreciate your perspective, but discussing politics during our time together creates unnecessary tension. Let's focus on enjoying each other's company instead."

Managing Pushback

Family members may not always respect the boundaries that non-bots set, especially if they feel their freedom to express their opinions is limited. Non-bots must be prepared for pushback and learn to reinforce their boundaries without escalating the situation.

Reaffirming Boundaries: If a family member continues to push past the boundary, non-bots should calmly reaffirm their position. For example, "I understand this topic is important to you, but I've asked that we avoid discussing it during family gatherings. Let's keep the conversation light."

Refusing to Engage: If a family member persists in discussing a contentious topic, non-bots can refuse to engage by simply not responding. Silence can be a powerful way to enforce boundaries without creating additional conflict.

Example: A non-bot has set a boundary about not discussing politics at family gatherings, but a relative repeatedly brings up a controversial topic. The non-bot calmly reaffirms the boundary, saying, "I've mentioned before that I'd rather not talk about this topic. Let's move on to something else." If the relative continues, the non-bot refuses to engage further, effectively shutting down the conversation.

Empathy as a Tool for Maintaining Connections

Empathy is a powerful tool that non-bots can use to maintain connections with family members, even when they disagree on important issues. By practicing empathy, non-bots can strengthen their family relationships, demonstrating that they care about their loved ones' feelings and experiences, even if they don't share their beliefs.

Practicing Empathy in Conversations

Empathy allows non-bots to see the world from their family members' perspectives, which can help defuse tension and foster understanding. Non-bots can use empathetic listening and responses to show their family members they are heard, even if they disagree with their viewpoints.

Listen Without Judgment: Non-bots can practice empathetic listening by allowing their family members to express their feelings and perspectives without immediately judging or responding. This creates a safe space for dialogue and can reduce the emotional charge of the conversation.

Acknowledge Emotions: Non-bots can acknowledge their family members' emotions, even if they disagree with the content of their beliefs. For example, a non-bot might say, "I can see that this issue matters to you," or "It sounds like you're feeling frustrated by this situation." This acknowledgment can help family members feel validated and reduce defensiveness.

Example: A non-bot's family member expresses frustration about a social issue, citing misinformation from the media. Rather than correcting the misinformation, the non-bot listens empathetically and acknowledges the family member's frustration by saying, "I can tell this is something you care a lot about." This response helps maintain the connection without escalating the conversation into an argument.

Finding Common Ground

Empathy also helps non-bots find common ground with their family members, which can strengthen relationships despite differing beliefs. By focusing on shared values and experiences, non-bots can maintain meaningful connections while avoiding contentious topics.

Shared Values: Non-bots can identify shared values or experiences with their family members that transcend political or social disagreements. For example, focusing on family, health, or personal achievements can create a sense of connection, even when more divisive topics are off the table.

Positive Interactions: Empathy fosters positive interactions, which can help non-bots maintain strong relationships with their family members. By emphasizing the importance of connection over debate, non-bots can create a more harmonious family dynamic.

Example: A non-bot and their family member disagree on a significant political issue but share a deep love for family traditions. By focusing on planning the next family reunion or reminiscing about shared memories, the non-bot strengthens their relationship despite the ideological divide.

Conclusion: Maintaining Family Harmony as a Non-Bot

Navigating family dynamics as a non-bot can be challenging, especially when family members are deeply attached to societal narratives. However, by avoiding confrontation, setting clear boundaries, and practicing empathy, non-bots can maintain harmony in their family relationships without sacrificing authenticity. These strategies allow non-bots to preserve emotional well-being while fostering meaningful connections with their loved ones. Family gatherings and interactions don't have to be a source of conflict—non-bots can create environments where understanding, respect, and love prevail, even in the face of differing beliefs.

Chapter 6
Navigating the Workplace

The workplace presents unique challenges for non-bots, who often find themselves in environments dominated by bots driven by conformity, office politics, and social dynamics. Navigating a bot-dominated workplace requires non-bots to maintain professionalism, avoid unnecessary conflict, and focus on results while blending in to avoid becoming a target. This chapter explores strategies for understanding workplace bots, blending in without sacrificing work ethic or integrity, and steering clear of gossip and controversial discussions to ensure success in the workplace.

Office Politics and Understanding Workplace Bots

Office politics can be one of the most challenging aspects of a bot-dominated workplace for non-bots. Bots often thrive when networking, alliances, and social maneuvering precede competence and results. To successfully navigate the workplace, non-bots must first understand bots' role in office politics and how to avoid getting caught up in the social dynamics that can undermine their professionalism and focus.

Understanding the Role of Bots in Office Politics

Bots in the workplace are often motivated by social acceptance, a desire for validation, and the need to fit in with the dominant workplace culture. They may engage in behaviors such as gossip, flattery, or forming cliques to gain favor with managers and colleagues. This behavior can be frustrating for non-bots, who prefer to focus on their work rather than engage in social maneuvering.

Bots Seeking Approval: Many workplace bots focus on gaining approval from their superiors and peers. They may prioritize pleasing their bosses or aligning with popular workplace opinions, even if it means compromising quality or ethics. Non-bots may find this behavior difficult to understand, especially when it leads to promotions or recognition for superficial reasons.

Cliques and Social Hierarchies: Bots often form cliques or social groups within the workplace, creating a hierarchy based on popularity rather than merit. Non-bots who value critical thinking and authenticity may feel out of place in these environments and struggle to navigate the complex social dynamics.

Example: In an office where a popular bot has become the manager's favorite through constant flattery, a non-bot might find it frustrating to see someone rise in the company through social maneuvering rather than hard work. Rather than directly confronting the unfairness, the non-bot must understand how to avoid being drawn into office politics while maintaining professionalism.

Avoiding Engagement in Office Politics

Non-bots must learn to disengage from office politics without isolating themselves from their colleagues. This can be achieved by maintaining a low profile in social maneuvering while focusing on results and professionalism. Non-bots who refuse to engage in gossip or flattery must balance blending in and preserving their authenticity.

Staying Neutral: In a bots-dominated workplace, neutrality can be a non-bot's best tool. By staying neutral in conversations about office politics, non-bots can avoid being drawn into cliques or taking sides in office rivalries. This keeps the non-bot from unnecessary conflicts and allows them to focus on their work.

Professional Distance: Non-bots should maintain a professional distance from colleagues heavily engaged in office politics. This doesn't mean isolating oneself completely but avoiding becoming too emotionally invested in workplace social dynamics. Maintaining a focus on work rather than personal relationships can help non-bots avoid the pitfalls of office politics.

Example: A non-bot in a workplace where two teams are vying for the manager's approval might choose to stay neutral by focusing on their work and avoiding conversations about team rivalry. By maintaining professional distance and staying focused on results, the non-bot can navigate office politics without becoming involved.

Blending In While Keeping Your Focus on Work and Results

Non-bots must learn to blend in with workplace culture without compromising their focus on work and results. While it's important to be sociable and get along with colleagues, non-bots should remain centered on their professional responsibilities and avoid getting distracted by the social dynamics that dominate bot-driven workplaces.

Staying Focused on Performance

One of the critical strengths non-bots can bring to the workplace is their focus on performance and results. In environments where bots may prioritize social status or workplace popularity, non-bots can stand out by consistently delivering high-quality work.

Letting Results Speak for Themselves: Rather than engaging in social maneuvering, non-bots should let their work speak for itself. By consistently delivering results, non-bots can build a reputation for reliability and competence that can help them succeed without relying on office politics.

Managing Expectations: While delivering strong performance is essential, non-bots should also be mindful of managing expectations. In workplaces where bots thrive on flattery or inflated promises, non-bots must set realistic expectations for their work and ensure that their performance meets or exceeds those expectations.

Example: A non-bot in a tech company may find that many colleagues focus on networking or gaining favor with senior management. Rather than getting involved in these social dynamics, the non-bot focuses on consistently delivering high-quality code and completing projects on time, which earns them recognition based on merit rather than social influence.

Blending In Without Compromising Values

Blending in doesn't mean sacrificing one's values or becoming part of the bot-dominated culture. Non-bots can learn to blend in socially while maintaining their commitment to professionalism and authenticity. This requires adapting to workplace norms without fully participating in the superficial behaviors that bots may prioritize.

Adopting Workplace Norms: Non-bots can adopt certain workplace norms—such as attending social events, participating in small talk, or using workplace jargon—without compromising their authenticity. By blending in with surface-level behaviors, non-bots can avoid drawing unnecessary attention to themselves while remaining true to their core values.

Selective Engagement: Non-bots should selectively engage in workplace social activities, choosing events or conversations that are more neutral or professional. This allows non-bots to maintain a presence in the workplace social scene without becoming overly involved in gossip or social rivalries.

Example: A non-bot working in a corporate office may attend occasional team-building events or happy hours to build rapport with colleagues. However, they avoid becoming deeply involved in personal conversations or workplace gossip, focusing on maintaining professionalism and building relationships based on mutual respect.

Avoiding Gossip and Controversial Discussions

Gossip and controversial discussions can be a significant source of conflict in the workplace, especially for non-bots who prefer to avoid emotional manipulation and misinformation. Bots may thrive on gossip to strengthen social bonds or gain social status. Still, non-bots should be cautious about engaging in these behaviors, as they can lead to unnecessary drama and distraction from work.

Steering Clear of Gossip

Gossip is a common feature of bot-dominated workplaces, where employees may spread rumors or speculate about colleagues' personal lives or professional performance. Non-bots should be mindful of the consequences of gossip and avoid becoming involved in these conversations.

The Consequences of Gossip: Gossiping can damage a non-bot's professional reputation and lead to strained colleague relationships. Even if the gossip seems harmless, it can contribute to a toxic workplace culture and create employee divisions.

Tactfully Avoiding Gossip: When faced with gossip in the workplace, non-bots can tactfully redirect the conversation or excuse themselves. For example, when colleagues gossip about a coworker, the non-bot might say, "I haven't heard about that," and change the subject to work-related topics. Alternatively, the non-bot can excuse themselves from the conversation altogether.

Example: A non-bot in a healthcare setting overhears colleagues gossiping about a coworker's personal life. Rather than joining the conversation, the non-bot redirects the discussion to a neutral topic, asking about upcoming projects or recent developments in the workplace.

Avoiding Controversial Discussions

In addition to gossip, controversial discussions about politics, religion, or other divisive topics can create tension in the workplace. Non-bots should avoid engaging in these conversations, as they can quickly escalate and lead to conflicts that disrupt workplace harmony.

Deflecting Controversial Topics: Non-bots can use deflection techniques to steer conversations away from controversial topics. For example, suppose a colleague brings up a political issue. In that case, the non-bot might respond with a neutral statement like, "I'm not sure this is the right place to discuss that," and redirect the conversation to a work-related matter.

Maintaining a Professional Focus: Non-bots should maintain a professional focus in workplace discussions, keeping conversations centered on work tasks, goals, and accomplishments. By avoiding emotionally charged topics, non-bots can protect their professional reputation and ensure that their interactions remain positive and productive.

Example: A non-bot working in an open-plan office overhears colleagues discussing a recent political event. When asked for their opinion, the non-bot responds, "I'm focused on this deadline right now, but I'd be happy to catch up on work after I finish." This response deflects the conversation without directly addressing the controversial topic.

Conclusion: Navigating the Workplace as a Non-Bot

Navigating a bot-dominated workplace requires non-bots to maintain professionalism, avoid getting drawn into office politics, and focus on delivering results. By understanding the dynamics of office politics, blending in with workplace norms, and avoiding gossip and controversial discussions, non-bots can maintain a solid professional presence while staying true to their values. These strategies allow non-bots to thrive in the workplace, building a reputation for competence and integrity without compromising authenticity.

Chapter 7

Public Interactions And Social Situations

Navigating public spaces and social situations can be challenging for non-bots, especially when bots dominate the conversations with emotionally charged debates, societal narratives, and groupthink. Whether it's a public debate at a social gathering or a casual interaction at a community event, non-bots must learn how to blend in, maintain their peace, and avoid unnecessary conflict. This chapter provides strategies for non-bots to remain neutral in public debates, use humor to defuse tension, and prevent emotional triggers during conversations in public spaces.

Staying Neutral in Public Debates

Public debates, especially on controversial topics, can quickly become emotionally charged, making it difficult for non-bots to participate without drawing unwanted attention or creating conflict. Staying neutral in these debates allows non-bots to engage socially without compromising their values or getting pulled into heated discussions.

The Importance of Neutrality

Neutrality offers non-bots a way to blend in with the crowd without fully engaging in the debate. By maintaining a neutral stance, non-bots can observe the conversation, gather insights, and participate when necessary without provoking a strong reaction from bots.

Avoiding Taking Sides: Bots often look for allies to reinforce their positions in public debates. Non-bots can avoid taking sides by using non-committal language such as, "That's an interesting point," or "I can see why you'd feel that way." This keeps the conversation neutral and allows the non-bot to participate without endorsing any particular viewpoint.

Maintaining Objectivity: Non-bots should focus on preserving objectivity during public debates, asking clarifying questions, and showing interest in understanding both sides of the issue. By asking open-ended questions like, "How did you come to that conclusion?" or "What are the sources for that information?" non-bots can stay engaged without committing to any position.

Example: A heated debate about climate change arises during a family reunion. A non-bot listens carefully without taking sides, occasionally offering neutral statements like, "It's a complicated issue with many perspectives." By staying neutral, the non-bot avoids being pulled into the emotional fray.

Observing Without Engaging

One of the most effective ways for non-bots to navigate public debates is to observe without engaging. By listening carefully, non-bots can gain insights into the emotional drivers of the conversation while avoiding the need to contribute their own opinions.

Active Listening: Non-bots can practice active listening by nodding, making brief comments like "Interesting" or "I hadn't thought of that," and letting others do most of the talking. This allows the non-bot to blend into the conversation without becoming a target of emotional reactions.

Resisting the Urge to Correct: In emotionally charged public debates, non-bots may be urged to correct misinformation or offer alternative perspectives. However, this can often lead to conflict. Non-bots can avoid escalating the situation by choosing to remain silent or offering neutral responses.

Example: A non-bot listens to both sides of the debate at a public forum discussing a local political issue without offering their opinion. When asked directly for their thoughts, the non-bot responds, "I'm still thinking it through—both sides have raised some good points." This keeps the non-bot from being drawn into the heated discussion.

Using Humor and Light-Heartedness to Defuse Tension

In public interactions, humor can be a powerful tool for defusing tension and maintaining a positive social atmosphere. By using light-heartedness and humor, non-bots can shift the tone of a conversation, allowing participants to relax and disengage from emotionally charged debates.

The Power of Humor in Social Situations

Humor helps break the intensity of emotionally charged discussions by offering a more relaxed and less aggressive way to engage with others. Humor can de-escalate conflict and bring levity to otherwise tense situations when used effectively.

Humor as a Distraction: When a public conversation becomes too intense or emotional, non-bots can use humor to distract from the heated topic. A well-timed joke or lighthearted comment can shift the focus of the conversation, allowing participants to take a step back from the debate.

Self-Deprecating Humor: Non-bots can also use self-deprecating humor to create a sense of camaraderie and reduce tension. By poking fun at themselves, non-bots can diffuse the seriousness of the conversation and make others feel more at ease.

Example: A discussion about a divisive political issue becomes increasingly tense at a party. Sensing the growing discomfort, the non-bot makes a lighthearted comment, "I'm still trying to figure out what the buttons on my microwave do—I'll leave politics to the experts!" This breaks the tension and shifts the conversation to a lighter tone.

Balancing Humor with Sensitivity

While humor can be an effective way to defuse tension, non-bots need to be mindful of the context and emotional state of the participants. Non-bots should avoid humor perceived as dismissive or mocking, especially when discussing sensitive topics.

Avoiding Sarcasm: Sarcasm can be easily misunderstood, especially in emotionally charged situations. Non-bots should avoid using sarcasm or humor that may come across as passive-aggressive or condescending. Instead, they should focus on light, playful humor that everyone can appreciate.

Reading the Room: Non-bots must be sensitive to the group's emotional state before introducing humor. If the conversation is too severe or participants are too emotionally invested, humor may not be appropriate. In such cases, non-bots should prioritize empathy and understanding over levity.

Example: During a heated conversation about healthcare policy at a work event, a non-bot senses that the room is too tense for humor. Instead of making a joke, the non-bot listens empathetically and offers a neutral comment like, "These are tough issues to figure out." This shows sensitivity to the emotional tone of the discussion.

Avoiding Emotional Triggers in Public Conversations

Public conversations trigger emotional triggers, especially when bots dominate discussions with societal narratives or controversial opinions. For non-bots, it's essential to recognize these triggers and avoid engaging in emotionally charged debates that can escalate into conflict.

Identifying Emotional Triggers

Emotional triggers in public conversations often arise when participants feel strongly about a particular issue or when their identity is closely tied to their beliefs. Non-bots should be aware of the topics or phrases likely to trigger emotional reactions in others.

Sensitive Topics: Discussions about politics, religion, and social justice issues are often emotionally charged and can quickly escalate if not handled carefully. Non-bots should be cautious when these topics arise in public settings and consider whether engaging in the conversation is worth the emotional toll.

Personal Attacks: Bots may respond to challenges by making personal attacks or using emotionally charged language. Non-bots should recognize when a conversation moves toward personal attacks and disengage before the situation escalates.

Example: At a community event, a non-bot overhears a conversation about immigration policy. Recognizing the potential for strong emotional reactions, the non-bot chooses not to engage in the discussion and instead joins a different group discussing a neutral topic like local sports.

Disengaging from Emotionally Charged Conversations

When a public conversation becomes emotionally charged, non-bots should disengage rather than escalate the situation. Disengagement can take many forms, from physically removing oneself from the conversation to redirecting the discussion toward less divisive topics.

Politely Excusing Oneself: If a conversation becomes too intense, non-bots can politely excuse themselves by saying something like, "I need to step away for a moment," or "I'll catch up with you later." This allows the non-bot to exit the conversation without causing further tension.

Redirecting the Conversation: If the non-bot feels that disengaging entirely is impossible, they can attempt to redirect the conversation to a less emotional topic. For example, if a debate about gun control arises, the non-bot might steer the conversation toward a related but less divisive topic like community safety initiatives.

Example: During a public debate at a neighborhood meeting, a non-bot notices the conversation about education reform becoming increasingly heated. Rather than engaging, the non-bot excuses themselves by saying, "I need to step out for a moment," and leaves the discussion before it escalates.

Maintaining Composure

Maintaining emotional composure is crucial when navigating emotionally charged public conversations. Non-bots can practice techniques like deep breathing, mindfulness, or emotional detachment to stay calm and centered, even when faced with intense emotional reactions from others.

Breathing Techniques: When a conversation becomes tense, non-bots can use breathing techniques to calm their nerves and avoid becoming emotionally reactive. Slow, deep breaths can help non-bots maintain composure and respond thoughtfully rather than impulsively.

Emotional Detachment: Non-bots can also practice emotional detachment by reminding themselves that the conversation is not a personal attack. By mentally distancing themselves from the emotional intensity of the discussion, non-bots can maintain a sense of inner calm and avoid reacting defensively.

Example: A non-bot attending a town hall meeting feels their pulse quicken as a participant makes a polarizing statement. The non-bot takes a few deep breaths, reminding themselves they don't need to engage emotionally. By maintaining composure, the non-bot avoids being drawn into the debate.

Conclusion: Thriving in Public Interactions

Navigating public interactions and social situations where bots dominate discussions requires non-bots to remain neutral, use humor to diffuse tension, and avoid emotional triggers. By staying neutral in public debates, non-bots can observe and participate without becoming targets of emotional reactions. Using humor and light-heartedness, non-bots can shift the tone of conversations, making them more enjoyable for everyone involved. Finally, by recognizing and avoiding emotional triggers, non-bots can protect their peace and control their interactions in public spaces.

These strategies allow non-bots to confidently engage in social and public interactions, ensuring that they maintain their authenticity while avoiding the emotional conflicts that often arise in bot-dominated environments.

Chapter 8

Self-Preservation and Mental Health

Living in a world dominated by bots can have a significant impact on the mental health of non-bots. Constantly being surrounded by individuals who conform to societal narratives can lead to frustration, emotional exhaustion, and feelings of isolation. This chapter explores the importance of maintaining mental clarity and protecting one's emotional well-being. We'll cover practical techniques for staying calm and centered, finding safe outlets for expressing true thoughts, and balancing authenticity with the need to adapt to emotionally challenging situations.

Techniques for Staying Calm and Centered

In a world filled with bots, non-bots often face emotionally charged conversations and interactions that can be overwhelming. Developing strategies to remain calm and centered is crucial for maintaining mental clarity and avoiding burnout.

Mindfulness Practices

Mindfulness is a powerful tool for helping non-bots remain calm and focused in stressful situations. By practicing mindfulness techniques, non-bots can learn to focus on the present moment, reducing the impact of external stressors.

Breathing Exercises: Deep breathing helps calm the nervous system and reduce feelings of stress. Non-bots can use this technique during intense conversations or after emotionally draining interactions to regain control of their mental state.

Body Awareness: A mindfulness practice that involves scanning the body for tension and consciously relaxing those areas can help non-bots stay calm. By focusing on the physical sensations in their body, non-bots can disconnect from overwhelming thoughts or emotions.

Example: A non-bot in a stressful work meeting uses a slow breathing technique to stay composed as a bot-driven conversation escalates. By focusing on their breath, the non-bot avoids reacting impulsively and remains centered throughout the meeting.

Emotional Detachment

Non-bots can protect their mental health by practicing emotional detachment. This involves learning to step back from emotionally charged situations and not allowing external factors to impact their internal peace.

Third-Person Perspective: Non-bots can imagine themselves as observers rather than participants in emotionally intense conversations. This technique creates a sense of distance from the situation, allowing non-bots to remain calm and objective.

Setting Emotional Boundaries: Emotional boundaries are critical for protecting one's mental well-being. Non-bots can decide in advance how much emotional energy they are willing to invest in conversations, helping them disengage when necessary.

Example: During a family argument, a non-bot steps back mentally, viewing the situation from a third-person perspective. By detaching from the emotional intensity of the argument, the non-bot remains calm and avoids being pulled into the conflict.

Grounding Techniques

Grounding techniques help non-bots stay connected to the moment when they feel overwhelmed. These techniques can prevent the mind from spiraling into anxiety or stress.

Five Senses Grounding: This technique focuses on what one can see, hear, touch, smell, and taste in the current environment. By engaging the senses, non-bots can return to the present and avoid emotional overwhelm.

Progressive Muscle Relaxation: Tensing and relaxing different muscle groups can help release physical tension and promote relaxation. Non-bots can use this technique to stay calm in high-stress environments.

Example: At a public event where tensions are high, a non-bot uses the five senses grounding technique to stay present. They focus on the sounds around them and the feel of their feet on the ground, which helps them remain composed despite the emotionally charged atmosphere.

Finding Outlets for Expressing Your True Thoughts

While non-bots often need to adapt and blend in with bots in public and professional settings, it's equally essential for them to find safe outlets to express their true thoughts and emotions. Without these outlets, non-bots may experience emotional exhaustion and frustration.

Creative Expression

Creative activities allow non-bots to channel their thoughts and emotions into art, writing, or music. This form of expression helps non-bots process their feelings in a private, non-judgmental space.

Journaling: Writing down thoughts and feelings is a powerful way to release pent-up emotions. Journaling provides a safe space for non-bots to be completely honest without fear of judgment.

Artistic Expression: Non-bots who enjoy drawing, painting, or creating music can use these outlets to express emotions that may be difficult to articulate. Creative expression offers a therapeutic way to process thoughts and feelings.

Example: After a difficult day at work, a non-bot takes some time to journal about their frustrations. This helps them release the emotions they had to suppress throughout the day, allowing them to process their feelings and feel more grounded.

Private Conversations with Trusted Individuals

A network of trusted individuals is essential for non-bots to maintain their emotional well-being. Close friends or family members who understand their perspective can provide a safe space for open, honest conversations.

Building a Support Network: Non-bots should cultivate relationships with people who share their values and can offer emotional support. These individuals provide a safe outlet for expressing true thoughts without fear of conflict.

One-on-One Conversations: Private, one-on-one conversations are often more productive than group discussions. Non-bots can have more profound, more meaningful conversations with trusted individuals where they can share their true feelings openly.

Example: After a heated family gathering, a non-bot calls a trusted friend to discuss their frustrations. The one-on-one conversation allows the non-bot to express their true feelings without the emotional intensity of the family setting.

Online and Anonymous Platforms

When non-bots feel isolated or lack local support, online communities can provide a safe space for self-expression. Anonymous platforms allow non-bots to connect with others without the fear of social repercussions.

Joining Online Communities: Non-bots can find online forums or communities to discuss with like-minded individuals. These spaces allow non-bots to express their thoughts freely, knowing they are in a supportive environment.

Anonymous Writing or Blogging: Writing anonymously offers non-bots a way to share their true thoughts and opinions without the pressure of being identified. This can be a liberating way for non-bots to express themselves.

Example: A non-bot who feels isolated in their local community joins an online forum where they can discuss societal issues with others who share their perspective. This anonymous platform gives them a safe outlet for expressing their true thoughts.

Balancing Authenticity with Adaptation in Emotionally Taxing Situations

Non-bots often face the challenge of balancing their authenticity with the need to adapt to socially or emotionally taxing environments. Maintaining this balance is crucial for protecting mental health while navigating bot-dominated spaces.

Knowing When to Adapt

Non-bots don't need to sacrifice their authenticity, but they should know when to adapt to social situations to avoid unnecessary conflict. This involves understanding when to remain neutral and when expressing one's true thoughts is appropriate.

Choosing Battles Wisely: Not every conversation requires full disclosure of one's beliefs. Non-bots should carefully choose when to engage and when to blend in to preserve social harmony and avoid emotional exhaustion.

Assessing the Social Environment: Non-bots should evaluate the emotional climate of a conversation before deciding whether to express their true thoughts. If the situation is emotionally charged or unlikely to lead to productive dialogue, it may be better to remain neutral.

Example: At a work event where the conversation turns political, a non-bot decides to remain neutral rather than share their views. They recognize that the environment is too emotionally charged for a productive discussion and prioritize maintaining workplace harmony.

Practicing Tactical Authenticity

Tactical authenticity involves expressing one's true self in measured and strategic ways based on the social context. This allows non-bots to maintain their authenticity without provoking emotional reactions from others.

Partial Disclosure: Non-bots can share parts of their perspective that are less likely to provoke defensiveness while keeping more controversial views private. This allows them to remain authentic without triggering conflict.

Finding Middle Ground: In some cases, non-bots can find common ground with bots by focusing on shared values or beliefs. This allows for a degree of authenticity while maintaining social harmony.

Example: In a conversation about social issues, a non-bot shares a moderate view that aligns with their core beliefs but avoids delving into their more controversial opinions. This allows them to contribute to the conversation without causing tension.

Conclusion: Balancing Mental Health and Authenticity in a Bot-Dominated World

Maintaining mental clarity and emotional well-being is essential for non-bots living in a bot-filled world. By practicing mindfulness, emotional detachment, and grounding techniques, non-bots can stay calm and centered in emotionally charged situations. Finding safe outlets for self-expression, whether through creative activities, private conversations, or online platforms, is crucial for maintaining authenticity without the constant pressure to adapt. Finally, non-bots can balance authenticity and adaptation by choosing when to express their true thoughts and practicing tactical authenticity in socially taxing environments.

By implementing these strategies, non-bots can protect their mental health while navigating bot-dominated spaces, preserving their emotional well-being and core values.

Chapter 9

Advanced Strategies for Challenging Situations

Non-bots often face difficult situations that test their emotional and mental resilience, especially when engaging with bots who may provoke, confront, or cause frustration. This chapter will explore advanced strategies to handle direct confrontations, deflect challenging questions, manage personal frustrations, and build supportive communities. By mastering these techniques, non-bots can navigate complex interactions with bots while maintaining their emotional and mental well-being.

Deflecting and Redirecting Challenging Questions

Non-bots are often confronted with challenging or provocative questions that can quickly lead to conflict if not handled skillfully. These questions are usually emotionally charged, designed to provoke a reaction or pin down a firm stance. Non-bots must learn the art of deflection and redirection to manage these conversations gracefully.

Using Non-Committal Responses

Non-committal responses allow non-bots to acknowledge a question without directly answering it or getting drawn into an emotionally charged discussion.

Neutral Acknowledgments: Phrases like, "That's an interesting point" or "I'll have to think more about that" allow non-bots to deflect challenging questions without giving a firm response. This keeps the conversation neutral and prevents escalation.

Avoiding Emotional Engagement: Non-bots can avoid emotionally charged conversations by remaining non-committal and steering clear of deep engagement with provocative topics.

Example: A non-bot is asked for their opinion on a controversial political issue at a social event. Instead of giving a direct answer, the non-bot responds, "I've heard so many different perspectives on that; it's a complex issue." This neutral response keeps the conversation from becoming heated.

Redirection as a Conversation Tool

Redirection involves steering the conversation from a contentious topic by introducing a related but less provocative subject. This technique helps non-bots avoid brutal confrontations while still engaging socially.

Shifting Focus: Non-bots can redirect the conversation by introducing a different angle or topic. For instance, if a bot asks a politically charged question, the non-bot can steer the conversation toward a more neutral aspect of the issue.

Framing the Question Differently: Non-bots can also reframe a provocative question in a way that invites thoughtful discussion without triggering emotional defensiveness. This helps guide the conversation toward a more constructive dialogue.

Example: During a dinner conversation, a bot asks a non-bot about their opinion on a polarizing issue. The non-bot reframes the question by saying, "I think what's more important is how we're all trying to find solutions that work for everyone. What solutions do you think could work?" This redirection helps avoid confrontation while keeping the conversation focused on solutions.

Disengaging from Confrontations

Sometimes, the best strategy is disengaging from a conversation that is becoming too intense or aggressive. Non-bots should recognize when a conversation has reached an unproductive point and exit gracefully.

Polite Exit: When a conversation becomes too aggressive, non-bots can politely excuse themselves by saying, "I think I'll leave this topic for another time, but I appreciate hearing your thoughts." This helps diffuse tension while allowing the non-bot to exit the conversation.

Physical Disengagement: In social settings, non-bots can physically disengage by changing location or redirecting their attention elsewhere. This strategy prevents further escalation and helps the non-bot regain mental clarity.

Example: A non-bot at a social event notices a conversation turning into a heated debate. Rather than engage further, they excuse themselves politely, saying, "I'm going to check in on something. It's been interesting hearing everyone's thoughts." This allows the non-bot to exit the situation without escalating the conflict.

Internal Coping Mechanisms for Managing Frustration

Living as a non-bot in a world filled with bots can be emotionally taxing. Frustration can build up over time as non-bots encounter uncritical thinking, emotional reactions, and societal conformity. To maintain mental health, non-bots need internal coping mechanisms to manage these frustrations effectively.

Identifying and Recognizing Triggers

Non-bots should first identify the triggers that cause frustration during interactions with bots. Recognizing these triggers allows non-bots to anticipate challenging situations and prepare strategies for staying calm.

Emotional Awareness: Non-bots should become aware of their physical and emotional responses to frustration, such as a racing heart, clenched muscles, or irritability. Recognizing these signs early can help non-bots intervene before their frustration escalates.

Pattern Recognition: By reflecting on past interactions, non-bots can identify patterns that trigger frustration. Whether it's specific topics, individuals, or environments, recognizing these patterns helps non-bots avoid unnecessary frustration.

Example: A non-bot notices that they become frustrated every time a particular family member brings up politics at gatherings. By identifying this pattern, the non-bot prepares strategies to avoid the conversation or stay calm during these moments.

Emotional Regulation Techniques

Managing frustration in real-time requires emotional regulation techniques that allow non-bots to maintain composure during challenging interactions.

Deep Breathing: Deep, controlled breathing can help non-bots manage feelings of frustration. By slowing their breathing, non-bots can reduce tension and regain emotional balance.

Cognitive Reframing: Reframing involves changing how non-bots think about a frustrating situation. Instead of viewing the interaction as a personal attack, non-bots can reframe it as an opportunity to practice patience or learn more about how bots think.

Example: During a tense conversation at work, a non-bot feels frustration building up. They take a few deep breaths and remind themselves that the conversation isn't personal but a reflection of the bot's emotional investment in the topic. This reframing helps the non-bot stay calm and continue the conversation without becoming defensive.

Managing Long-Term Stress

Beyond managing immediate frustrations, non-bots must develop strategies to handle the long-term stress of living in a bot-dominated world. Maintaining emotional balance over time requires building habits that promote mental well-being.

Physical Exercise: Regular physical activity is a proven way to reduce stress and release tension. Non-bots can incorporate exercise, such as walking, yoga, or running, into their routine to help manage the cumulative effects of stress.

Mindfulness and Meditation: Practicing mindfulness or meditation helps non-bots stay grounded and maintain mental clarity. These practices create moments of stillness, allowing non-bots to reset emotionally and avoid burnout.

Example: A non-bot who frequently deals with stressful work situations incorporates a daily 15-minute mindfulness practice into their morning routine. This helps them start the day with a clear mind and better equips them to handle frustrations throughout the day.

Building Supportive Communities of Like-Minded Individuals

Navigating the challenges of a bot-dominated world is much easier when non-bots have a supportive community of like-minded individuals. Finding people with similar values and perspectives provides non-bots with a safe space for authentic expression and emotional support.

Finding Like-Minded Individuals

Non-bots should actively seek out individuals or groups that share their values, beliefs, and perspectives. These connections provide much-needed validation and create a sense of belonging.

Joining Communities: Non-bots can join local or online communities that align with their views, such as interest groups, discussion forums, or clubs. These spaces allow non-bots to engage in meaningful conversations without the pressure to conform to societal norms.

Forming Trust-Based Relationships: Building relationships with like-minded individuals takes time and trust. Non-bots should seek people who demonstrate empathy, understanding, and mutual respect.

Example: A non-bot joins a local book club where the members discuss philosophical ideas and question societal narratives. Over time, the non-bot forms close relationships with several members, finding a safe space to share their thoughts and frustrations.

Creating Safe Spaces for Expression

Safe spaces—whether online or in person—allow non-bots to express their thoughts without fear of judgment or conflict. These spaces are essential for emotional well-being, allowing non-bots to decompress and reflect.

Private Gatherings: Non-bots can create safe spaces by organizing private gatherings with trusted friends. These small, intimate settings allow non-bots to engage in open discussions without the emotional intensity of larger, bot-dominated environments.

Online Platforms: For non-bots who feel isolated, online platforms offer a valuable outlet for self-expression. Engaging with like-minded individuals in online forums or discussion groups can provide a sense of community and support.

Example: A non-bot starts hosting monthly dinners with a few close friends where they can openly discuss societal issues and support one another. These gatherings provide a safe space for the non-bot to express their thoughts without the pressure of conforming to societal norms.

Conclusion: Navigating Challenging Situations as a Non-Bot

Advanced strategies for handling challenging situations allow non-bots to navigate confrontations, provocative questions, and personal frustrations while maintaining emotional balance. By mastering the art of deflection and redirection, non-bots can gracefully handle confrontational moments without engaging in heated debates. Internal coping mechanisms, such as deep breathing and cognitive reframing, help non-bots manage frustration at the moment and prevent long-term stress. Finally, building supportive communities of like-minded individuals provides non-bots with the emotional support and validation they need to thrive in a bot-filled world.

Chapter 10

Conclusion and Final Thoughts

As non-bots navigate a world dominated by societal norms, emotionally driven narratives, and uncritical thinking, they face unique challenges in maintaining authenticity and emotional well-being. However, with the right strategies, non-bots can survive and thrive, finding a path to remain true to their values while adapting to the pressures of bot-dominated environments. This concluding chapter will recap key strategies, offer encouragement to continue the pursuit of truth and emphasize the importance of maintaining hope and balance.

Surviving and Thriving in a Bot-Filled World

One of the most significant challenges for non-bots is maintaining mental clarity and emotional balance while navigating an overwhelming world. However, through the strategies covered in this book—such as blending in without compromising values, practicing mindfulness, and building supportive communities—non-bots have the tools to succeed.

Adapting Without Losing Authenticity

Non-bots must adapt to bot-dominated environments, but this adaptation does not mean sacrificing one's core beliefs or authenticity. Using techniques such as tactical authenticity and selective engagement, non-bots can balance maintaining their inner truth and blending into social and professional spaces.

Blending in for Survival: In many social and professional settings, blending in is necessary for survival. Non-bots can use the strategies outlined in this book—such as mirroring, diplomatic language, and active listening—to avoid confrontation while preserving their integrity.

Choosing Battles: Non-bots should carefully choose when to express their true thoughts and when to remain neutral. Not every conversation requires full disclosure of beliefs, and sometimes, the best strategy is to remain silent or offer non-committal responses to preserve harmony.

Example: A non-bot working in a corporate office uses diplomatic language to navigate a tense meeting, choosing to remain neutral on a controversial issue while staying focused on the work. By blending in, the non-bot avoids unnecessary conflict while maintaining their professionalism.

Thriving Through Self-Care and Connection

Thriving as a non-bot requires more than surviving challenging interactions; it involves maintaining one's emotional and mental health through self-care and connection with like-minded individuals. Non-bots must prioritize their well-being, using techniques like mindfulness, exercise, and creative expression to maintain emotional balance.

Practicing Self-Care: Mindfulness practices like meditation and grounding exercises help non-bots stay centered in emotionally charged environments.

Physical activity and creative expression also provide essential outlets for releasing tension and maintaining mental clarity.

Building a Supportive Network: Non-bots should seek out communities of like-minded individuals, whether in person or online, to provide emotional support and validation. These connections help non-bots maintain authenticity and offer a safe space to express their thoughts.

Example: After a difficult week at work, a non-bot attends a small gathering with close friends who share their values. The supportive environment allows the non-bot to decompress and recharge, helping them maintain their emotional balance and thrive in a bot-filled world.

Maintaining Hope and Inspiring Others to Seek Truth

While it can be challenging to live in a world where bots dominate the conversation, non-bots should not lose hope. Pursuing truth and critical thinking is valuable, even if it sometimes feels isolating. Non-bots have the potential to inspire others—both bots and non-bots alike—to think more critically and seek the truth for themselves.

The Ripple Effect of Critical Thinking

Non-bots may feel that their efforts to inspire change or encourage critical thinking are often resisted. However, even small actions can have a ripple effect, planting seeds of doubt or curiosity in bots entrenched in societal narratives.

Planting Seeds of Curiosity: By using subtle influence techniques—such as asking thought-provoking questions or gently challenging assumptions—non-bots can create opportunities for others to reconsider their beliefs.

Leading by Example: Non-bots can inspire others simply by living authentically and demonstrating critical thinking daily. Their actions, rather than words, can be a powerful example to those around them.

Example: A non-bot asks a thoughtful question during a family discussion about a societal issue, gently encouraging their relatives to consider a different perspective. Although the conversation doesn't change immediately, the non-bot knows they've planted a seed of curiosity that may grow over time.

Maintaining Hope Amid Challenges

It can be challenging for non-bots to remain hopeful when they face constant resistance from bots or feel overwhelmed by societal pressures. However, maintaining hope is crucial for emotional well-being and continuing the pursuit of truth.

Focusing on Long-Term Change: Non-bots should remember that societal change is slow. While individual conversations may not always yield immediate results, the cumulative effect of questioning societal norms can lead to greater awareness and change over time.

Recognizing Small Wins: Non-bots should celebrate small victories, such as successfully navigating a difficult conversation without conflict or inspiring a single person to think more critically. These small wins motivate the pursuit of truth, even in the face of resistance.

Example: After a challenging day at work where they felt surrounded by bots, a non-bot reflects on a recent conversation in which they successfully encouraged a colleague to question a common misconception. This small win helps the non-bot remain hopeful about the long-term impact of their efforts.

Finding Balance Between Adaptation and Authenticity

One of the central themes of this book is the importance of finding balance—between blending in and staying true to oneself, between adapting to social pressures and maintaining integrity. Non-bots must navigate this delicate balance in their daily lives, ensuring they can function within bot-dominated environments without sacrificing their core values.

The Adaptation-Acceptance Spectrum

Living authentically in a world of bots doesn't mean rejecting adaptation altogether. Non-bots should view adaptation as a survival and social harmony tool while prioritizing their own mental and emotional well-being.

Adapting Strategically: Non-bots can adapt strategically to different environments, choosing to blend in when necessary but maintaining their authenticity in spaces where they feel safe and supported. This approach ensures that non-bots can navigate societal pressures without feeling overwhelmed or isolated.

Preserving Integrity: Even while adapting, non-bots should be mindful of maintaining their integrity. This means staying true to their values and beliefs in situations where authenticity is essential and only adapting when it serves a clear purpose, such as avoiding unnecessary conflict.

Example: A non-bot blends in during a heated political discussion at a family gathering, offering neutral responses to avoid conflict. Later, in a private conversation with a trusted friend, the non-bot expresses their true thoughts more openly. By adapting strategically, the non-bot maintains social harmony while preserving its authenticity.

Conclusion: Continuing the Journey as a Non-Bot

Navigating a bot-filled world is difficult, but non-bots have the strength, resilience, and tools to survive and thrive. By implementing the strategies outlined in this book—blending in when necessary, practicing emotional regulation, building supportive communities, and maintaining hope—, non-bots can protect their mental and emotional well-being while continuing the pursuit of truth.

Remember, you are not alone in this journey. Others share your values and critical thinking skills. By connecting with like-minded individuals and inspiring others to seek truth, you are contributing to a more aware and thoughtful society. The path of a non-bot may be challenging. Still, it is a path worth walking—leading to deeper understanding, personal growth, and, ultimately, preserving your authenticity in a world that often values conformity.

Keep questioning, seek truth, and remember that your journey as a non-bot is valuable and necessary.

Biblical Perspective Spiritual Blindness and Awakening: A Biblical Perspective

The Bible contains timeless teachings on spiritual blindness, ignorance, and conformity—issues that closely parallel the modern concept of "bots." As non-bots today struggle to interact with those who cling to falsehoods or unthinkingly follow societal narratives, the prophets, and Jesus confronted similar dynamics in their time. This chapter explores how biblical prophecies, teachings, and stories offer wisdom that resonates with the experience of living among spiritually asleep individuals. By drawing these connections, we understand how spiritual blindness has always been a challenge for humanity and how awakening remains the solution.

Old Testament Foundations: Prophecies of Spiritual Blindness and Rebellion

Isaiah's Call to a Spiritually Blind People (Isaiah 6:9-10)

The prophet Isaiah was called to deliver a complex message to Israel, a nation that had become spiritually blind and deaf to God's truth. In Isaiah 6:9-10, God commissions him to speak to people who "hear but do not understand" and "see but do not perceive." Despite being exposed to divine revelation, the Israelites remained unmoved, their hearts hardened to the truth.

This mirrors the experience of non-bots today, who engage with individuals—modern-day bots—who hear and see the truth but refuse to acknowledge it. Isaiah's message reveals the consequences of spiritual blindness: stagnation, rebellion, and a deepening separation from divine revelation.

Spiritual Consequences: Spiritual blindness leads to a cycle of ignorance and rebellion. When people resist truth, they fall into deeper levels of misunderstanding, perpetuating ignorance that keeps them from transformation.

Example: Bots who cling to societal norms or false narratives are much like the Israelites, unable to perceive deeper truths due to their attachment to comfort and conformity.

Ezekiel's Message to the Rebellious House (Ezekiel 12:2)

In Ezekiel 12:2, the prophet addresses Israel's rebellion: "Son of man, you are living among a rebellious people. They have eyes to see but do not see and ears to hear but do not hear." This message underscores the active rejection of divine truth. Israel's refusal to heed the words of the prophets was not due to a lack of exposure to truth but rather a willful rebellion against it.

Today, bots exhibit this same dynamic by rejecting critical thinking and insight in favor of comfortable falsehoods. Like the Israelites, they choose ignorance over awareness, even when presented with evidence that challenges their beliefs.

Rebellion Against Truth: Spiritual blindness is not merely a passive state of ignorance but often an active rejection of truth. Bots, much like the Israelites, are not simply unaware—they choose to remain spiritually blind by clinging to societal lies and superficial narratives.

New Testament Teachings: Jesus and the Spiritually Blind

Blind Guides Leading the Blind (Matthew 15:14)

In Matthew 15:14, Jesus warns his disciples about the religious leaders of his day, calling them "blind guides." He explains that if "the blind lead the blind, both will fall into a pit." This metaphor illustrates the danger of spiritual blindness and conformity. Religious leaders, who were supposed to guide the people, had themselves become blind to the deeper truths of God's kingdom.

This teaching directly applies to modern-day bots, who, following unexamined beliefs or misinformation, lead others astray. Jesus' words emphasize the importance of discernment and critical thinking. Non-bots must be cautious not to follow the crowd unthinkingly but instead seek out truth intentionally.

Discernment in a World of Conformity: Jesus teaches the necessity of discernment in avoiding the pitfalls of societal conformity. Just as the disciples were called to recognize and reject blind guides, non-bots must develop the capacity to discern the truth amidst the noise of falsehood and misinformation.

Straining a Gnat, Swallowing a Camel (Matthew 23:24)

In Matthew 23:24, Jesus rebukes the Pharisees for their misplaced priorities, saying: "Blind guides! You strain out a gnat but swallow a camel." This powerful metaphor highlights the Pharisees' focus on minor, superficial details of religious observance while neglecting the larger truths of justice, mercy, and faithfulness.

Modern-day bots often engage in spiritual blindness, adhering strictly to societal rules and narratives while ignoring the deeper moral and spiritual truths that demand attention. Bots may focus on trivial matters, such as material success or social status while overlooking issues like compassion, integrity, and personal growth.

Hypocrisy and Ignorance: Like the Pharisees, Bots engage in spiritual blindness by adhering to the superficial while neglecting the essential. They follow societal rules without recognizing the deeper truths that define genuine spiritual and moral wisdom.

Jesus Healing the Physically and Spiritually Blind (John 9:1-7)

In John 9:1-7, Jesus heals a man born blind, providing a literal and metaphorical example of spiritual awakening. Jesus, as the world's light, brings vision to those living in spiritual darkness. His miracles are more than physical healings; they symbolize the more profound awakening when people come to know the truth and embrace it.

Non-bots, much like Jesus, seek to awaken others from spiritual blindness. Through patience, empathy, and truth-telling, non-bots can help others see beyond societal deception and ignorance.

Awakening the Spiritually Blind: Jesus' ministry focused on awakening the spiritually blind, offering light and truth to those in darkness. Modern-day non-bots are called beacons of truth in a world that clings to falsehood, much like Jesus provided spiritual vision to those unable to see.

Spiritual Blindness in Contemporary Society

Conformity and Spiritual Apathy: Modern Parallels to Biblical Warnings

Many people today live in a state of spiritual apathy, mirroring the spiritual blindness of the Israelites and Pharisees. Modern society's obsession with materialism, political correctness, and unquestioning loyalty to societal norms reflects the same apathy toward truth that biblical figures warned against.

Bots, content with their superficial beliefs and lifestyles, are often unwilling to seek deeper spiritual truths. Like the spiritually blind individuals of Jesus' time, they choose comfort over the hard work of awakening and transformation.

Bots as the "Walking Dead" (Ephesians 2:1-2)

Ephesians 2:1-2 describes those "dead in their transgressions and sins," offering a biblical parallel to the modern-day concept of bots. Though physically alive, bots are spiritually disconnected from the truth of God. They live in ignorance, following the patterns of the world without questioning or seeking more profound meaning.

Spiritual Death and Awakening: Just as the Bible describes those living in sin as spiritually dead, modern-day bots are alive physically but dead spiritually. Jesus' teachings offer a path out of this spiritual death through repentance, awakening, and redemption.

Jesus' Message for Non-Bots: Awakening the Spiritually Blind

Jesus' Compassion for the Spiritually Blind

Throughout his ministry, Jesus approached those living in spiritual blindness with compassion and a desire for their awakening. Non-bots can emulate Jesus' attitude in their interactions with bots by demonstrating patience, empathy, and a commitment to guiding others toward truth.

Calling for Repentance and Transformation (Mark 1:15)

Jesus' first public message was a call to repentance: "Repent, for the kingdom of heaven has come near" (Mark 1:15). This call to transformation is just as relevant for modern-day bots, who must turn away from societal falsehoods and embrace the truth. Non-bots can take inspiration from Jesus, offering truth and guidance to those willing to listen.

The Parable of the Sheep and Goats (Matthew 25:31-46)

In the Parable of the Sheep and Goats, Jesus separates those who are spiritually aware (the sheep) from those who are spiritually blind (the goats). Non-bots are called to embody the attributes of the sheep—following Christ's teachings with compassion, discernment, and commitment to truth.

Breaking Free from the Herd Mentality (Romans 12:2)

Romans 12:2 urges believers not to conform to the patterns of this world but to be transformed by renewing their minds. Like Jesus' followers, non-bots are called to resist societal pressure and instead pursue a transformed mind through truth and spiritual enlightenment.

Spreading Light in Darkness (Matthew 5:14-16)

Jesus calls his followers "the light of the world" (Matthew 5:14-16). Non-bots, aware of societal deception, are tasked with spreading this light and helping others see the truth. Just as Jesus illuminated the path for the spiritually blind, non-bots are called to guide others toward spiritual awakening.

Offering a Path to Redemption

Just as Jesus offered redemption to those in spiritual darkness, non-bots can offer insights and guidance for those willing to awaken from societal conformity. While awakening cannot be forced, non-bots can provide the tools and truth necessary for those ready to embrace a path of transformation.

Conclusion: Following Jesus' Example in a World of Bots

In conclusion, biblical teachings on spiritual blindness offer profound insights into the modern-day phenomenon of bots. Just as Jesus confronted spiritual blindness with patience, empathy, and truth, non-bots are called to do the same. By living authentically, seeking truth, and offering compassion to those trapped in ignorance, non-bots can play a vital role in awakening others from the darkness of societal deception and spiritual apathy.

Non-bots are responsible for embodying Christ's teachings—becoming beacons of light in a world filled with conformity and falsehood. Like Jesus, who healed the spiritually blind and called for transformation, non-bots must extend the same compassion and guidance, offering insight to those ready to break free from societal norms and embrace a deeper understanding of truth.

In a world where spiritual blindness continues to dominate, non-bots must remain steadfast in their commitment to truth, challenge conformity, and act with patience and discernment. As the Bible teaches, awakening the spiritually blind requires persistence, love, and wisdom. By following Jesus' example, non-bots can create a ripple effect of enlightenment, helping others see the world more clearly and embrace the freedom that comes with spiritual awakening.

Ultimately, the journey of awakening requires resilience. But as Jesus showed, even in a world of resistance and misunderstanding, it is possible to bring light to those in darkness. Non-bots must continue to shine their light, fostering truth and spiritual growth in those around them, even if the path is met with opposition.

The Influence of Material Wealth The Influence of Material Wealth on Perceptions of Validity

Material wealth and social status often dictate how individuals' ideas and insights are perceived in today's world. This chapter has explored the psychological and societal reasons why bots—those who cling to societal norms and misinformation—often dismiss non-bots' opinions, particularly when they lack material wealth or status symbols. The following sections delved into the power of wealth, status symbols, cognitive biases, and the consequences for dialogue and truth-seeking.

The Power of Material Wealth in Shaping Perceptions

Wealth as a Sign of Success and Authority

Bots rely heavily on material wealth and status symbols as a shorthand for success, authority, and credibility. This chapter explained how the halo effect and societal conditioning reinforce this dynamic, making it difficult for non-bots to be heard or taken seriously.

Cultural Conditioning Around Wealth

Society's long-standing tradition of celebrating financial success creates a cognitive barrier for bots, leading them to ignore or marginalize non-bots who do not conform to the image of material success. The chapter illustrated how cultural conditioning biases bots toward valuing wealth over substance, ultimately shaping how ideas are perceived and discussed.

The Influence of Status Symbols on Credibility

The Illusion of Expertise

Luxury status symbols create an illusion of expertise in areas where wealth may not translate into actual knowledge. Bots mistake material success for intelligence or wisdom, leading them to dismiss the contributions of non-bots who lack such visible markers of wealth.

The Role of Media in Reinforcing Wealth-Credibility Dynamics

The media reinforces this dynamic by frequently elevating wealthy voices in public discourse. Bots, in turn, absorb these narratives and are more likely to dismiss individuals who do not display wealth, even when they possess more excellent knowledge or expertise.

The Psychological Barriers to Accepting Non-Wealthy Individuals' Insights
Cognitive Biases and the Wealth-Ideas Disconnect

Cognitive biases like the halo effect and status quo bias make it difficult for bots to accept non-bot insights. These biases prevent bots from engaging meaningfully with ideas that challenge their preconceived notions about success and wealth.

The Fear of Challenging Societal Norms

For bots, accepting insights from a non-bot without wealth challenges the very societal structures they've come to rely on. This cognitive dissonance leads bots to dismiss or reject valuable ideas to avoid disrupting their worldview.

The Consequences of Dialogue and Truth-Seeking

When wealth is used as a credibility metric, it hinders meaningful dialogue and undermines the pursuit of truth. Prioritizing material wealth over knowledge and substance perpetuates misinformation and reinforces existing social inequalities. Non-bots who offer valuable insights are often silenced or marginalized, limiting the depth and diversity of conversations in both public and private spheres.

Conclusion: Moving Beyond Materialism to Truth-Seeking

The overemphasis on material wealth as a marker of validity damages the quality of public discourse and limits the spread of valuable ideas. Bots' tendency to equate wealth with credibility perpetuates a cycle where only wealthy voices dominate, sidelining the insights of non-bots, who often bring critical perspectives that could foster greater understanding and growth.

Moving beyond this materialistic framework is essential for fostering a more inclusive and intellectually honest society. Non-bots must continue to engage in dialogue with courage and conviction despite the challenges posed by societal norms. Encouraging critical thinking and a focus on the substance of ideas—rather than the material wealth of the speaker—is essential to creating an environment where truth-seeking can flourish.

In a world increasingly shaped by superficial markers of success, it is imperative to promote an understanding that wisdom, insight, and value do not depend on wealth. A more diverse and equitable exchange of ideas will benefit all, leading to more meaningful conversations, better solutions to societal problems, and a richer collective understanding of the world. By shifting focus from materialism to the merit of knowledge and insight, society can elevate truth over superficial status markers, leading to more genuine, productive, and thoughtful dialogue.

Encouragement for the Future
Encouragement for the Future

As we conclude this exploration into navigating a world filled with bots and those resistant to truth, we must reflect on the road ahead and the role each of us plays in shaping a more informed and connected society. The journey is far from over, and while challenges remain, this chapter aims to provide encouragement, motivation, and a reaffirmation of the critical role that perseverance, hope, and proactive engagement play in fostering a better future.

Embracing the Challenge

Living and engaging in a world where misinformation, resistance, and emotional entrenchment are common can feel daunting. It is easy to become discouraged by the magnitude of the task or the sheer volume of interactions with those who refuse to question or reflect on their beliefs. Yet, it is within these challenges that opportunity arises. Non-bots committed to truth, critical thinking, and understanding have a unique role to play in fostering a more aware and discerning society.

The Power of Patience and Resilience: The challenge of interacting with bots and resistant individuals requires patience. Non-bots must develop resilience to withstand the emotional toll of these interactions while remaining focused on encouraging thought and dialogue. It is crucial to remember that personal and societal growth often happens slowly and incrementally.

Transforming Challenges into Opportunities: Every difficult conversation, every moment of resistance, is an opportunity for learning and impact. These challenges offer a chance to refine your approach, strengthen your resolve, and influence others directly or indirectly. Even when immediate change seems unlikely, your effort to engage thoughtfully and authentically has the potential to plant seeds of critical thinking that may grow over time.

Example: A non-bot faces repeated resistance from family members when discussing important issues like societal inequality or misinformation in the media. While it may seem that no progress is being made, these conversations might open minds, create subtle shifts in perspective, or encourage more open dialogue within the family over time.

Cultivating Hope

Hope is essential to any effort to foster meaningful change. Change is possible even in a world filled with bots, where misinformation and emotional resistance seem to dominate. History has shown that shifts in understanding and awareness often begin with individuals who dare to challenge the status quo and ask difficult questions. As a non-bot, your role in creating this change is invaluable.

Incremental Progress is Meaningful: It's easy to feel overwhelmed by the scale of society's problems, but it's important to remember that progress is often incremental. Each conversation and moment of engagement contributes to a more significant movement toward greater awareness. Your efforts may seem small at the moment, but they have the potential to create ripples of change that extend far beyond your immediate interactions.

Finding Positivity in Small Victories: Instead of focusing solely on your resistance, look for moments of progress and growth in yourself and others. These small victories, whether a slight shift in someone's perspective or a deeper understanding of your approach, are essential. By focusing on what is possible rather than what seems impossible, you cultivate hope and motivation for the journey ahead.

Example: After several conversations with a close friend who had previously dismissed any discussion about societal issues, a non-bot notices the friend beginning to ask more questions and express curiosity. Though the friend may not have entirely changed their perspective, this subtle shift signifies progress and hope.

Staying True to Your Values

Navigating interactions with bots and those resistant to truth often requires adaptation and flexibility, but non-bots must remain grounded in their core values. Authenticity is a powerful force in fostering genuine connections and promoting meaningful dialogue.

Adaptation Without Compromise: While blending in and adapting to different environments to engage effectively, staying true to your core beliefs is essential. When you maintain your principles, you create an authentic and credible presence that can inspire others.

Authenticity as a Tool for Connection: People are often drawn to those who are genuine and consistent in their beliefs and actions. By staying true to your values, you create the potential for deeper connections and more honest conversations. Even bots, who may initially resist your perspective, are more likely to respect and engage with you when they sense that you are being authentic.

Example: A non-bot in a professional setting faces pressure to conform to the majority opinion on a controversial issue. Instead of compromising their beliefs, they find a way to express their perspective calmly and respectfully, maintaining their integrity while fostering a more open dialogue in the workplace.

Building Supportive Networks

The journey of fostering understanding and encouraging truth is not one you need to take alone. Finding and building supportive networks of like-minded individuals can give you the encouragement, validation, and shared wisdom required to stay focused and resilient. In these communities, you'll find strength, inspiration, and the motivation to continue engaging with the world positively and productively.

Seek Like-Minded Communities: There are countless groups, both online and in-person, where individuals committed to truth, critical thinking, and meaningful dialogue come together to support one another. Whether through forums, discussion groups, or local organizations, these networks can provide the solidarity and encouragement you need to remain resilient in your efforts.

Share Wisdom and Learn from Others: Engaging with others who share your values creates opportunities for learning and growth. By exchanging ideas, strategies, and experiences, you expand your understanding of navigating complex interactions and foster meaningful change in the world around you.

Example: A non-bot joins an online forum promoting critical thinking and dialogue around societal issues. Through discussions with others, they find new approaches for engaging with resistant individuals in their own lives and draw strength from the collective support of the group.

Contributing to Future Generations

One of the most meaningful aspects of the non-bot journey is your impact on future generations. By promoting critical thinking, fostering honest dialogue, and modeling the values of truth and discernment, you help lay the foundation for a more informed and cohesive society.

Mentorship and Guidance: Through direct mentorship or leading through example, non-bots can influence younger individuals. By encouraging them to value discernment and truth, you are helping to shape a future where critical thinking is more widely embraced and practiced.

Leaving a Legacy of Truth: Your actions today contribute to a more significant movement that will have ripple effects on future generations. Continuing to engage thoughtfully and with integrity creates a legacy that others will build upon. The seeds of truth you plant now will grow into a more connected and aware society.

Example: A non-bot discusses current events and critical thinking with their younger siblings or children. By encouraging them to question narratives and seek truth, the non-bot helps instill values that will guide the younger generation as they navigate their challenges in the future.

Final Reflections

As you move forward, it's essential to remember that the journey of fostering understanding and bridging divides is ongoing. The strategies and tools discussed in this book are just the beginning—they are meant to be practiced, refined, and applied consistently over time. Your impact may not always be immediate or visible, but your influence on those around you is accurate and significant.

Continuing the Work: Navigating a bot-filled world and promoting truth is continuous. Stay committed to your values, remain open to learning, and persist in engaging meaningfully with others. The road ahead may be challenging, but it is filled with opportunities for growth, connection, and positive change.

Embracing Growth and Learning: Every conversation and interaction is an opportunity to grow personally and in your understanding of others. Keep striving for clarity, compassion, and connection, knowing that your efforts are part of a more significant movement toward a more informed, honest, and connected world.

Conclusion: A Future of Hope and Impact

The path ahead is not without its difficulties but is also filled with promise. As a non-bot, your commitment to truth, integrity, and meaningful dialogue has the power to inspire and influence those around you. Embrace the challenges you face, knowing that your efforts contribute to a more significant movement of awakening and awareness.

By staying true to your values, cultivating hope, and building supportive networks, you will continue to make a meaningful impact on the world. Your dedication to fostering understanding and promoting truth shapes the present and paves the way for future generations to live in a more connected, informed, and compassionate society.

Keep moving forward with determination and optimism, knowing that your efforts make a difference, one conversation at a time.

Why I Chose the Term "Bot" to Describe Ignorant and Naïve Individuals Why I Chose the Term "Bot" to Describe Ignorant and Naïve Individuals

In a world filled with societal pressures, misinformation, and a constant flow of superficial narratives, it becomes increasingly difficult for many individuals to maintain a sense of individuality, curiosity, and critical thinking. This chapter delves into why I chose the term "bot" to describe those who, either through ignorance, naivety, or willful blindness, conform to these pressures and lose their ability to think independently. The term "bot" encapsulates the uniform, robotic-like behavior many exhibit as they parrot what they see and hear without questioning or challenging the status quo. Through this chapter, I'll explore the reasoning behind this choice, the behaviors that define a "bot," and how this term illustrates the contrast between bots and non-bots in today's society.

The Behavior of Bots: Repetition Without Thought

The term "bot" was chosen primarily because of the way individuals in this category act and respond. Much like automated computer programs, bots respond uniformly to stimuli. They absorb information from mass media, social media, and societal influences without critically analyzing or questioning it. They mirror the ideas, behaviors, and opinions of others without taking the time to think for themselves.

Uniformity in Thought and Response

Bots exhibit a striking uniformity in the way they react to the world. Whether discussing politics, religion, or social issues, their responses often sound rehearsed, as if they are repeating a script fed to them by the media or popular culture. This uniformity is critical to understanding why "bot" fits so well. Much like a programmed robot, they have a set number of predictable and unchanging responses.

Mimicking Media and Social Norms: Bots adopt the language, mannerisms, and beliefs they are exposed to, particularly from television, social media influencers, and mainstream narratives. Rather than developing original thoughts, they mimic what is presented, rarely questioning its validity or exploring alternative perspectives.

Loss of Individuality: The bot's behavior erases individuality. Bots are more focused on fitting in and aligning with what is considered socially acceptable, which causes them to lose touch with their true selves. The lack of curiosity or critical thinking results in robotic uniformity, hence the term "bot."

Example: During political discussions, bots often repeat talking points they've heard on the news or from public figures, regardless of whether they've fact-checked the information or truly understand its implications. This repetitive, unoriginal behavior mirrors how bots in programming follow preset instructions without deviation.

Ignorance and Laziness as the Foundation

Ignorance and laziness significantly affect why many people exhibit bot-like behavior. It is not necessarily a lack of intelligence but rather an unwillingness to engage with the world on a deeper level. Many bots remain ignorant because it is easier to accept the information they are given than to question it. The mental effort required to research, think critically, and challenge deeply held beliefs is often more than they are willing to invest.

The Comfort of Ignorance: Ignorance provides a sense of comfort and security. Bots avoid the discomfort of challenging their worldview or the fear that they may have been wrong in their beliefs. Instead of seeking truth, they embrace the safety of conformity and societal approval.

Laziness in Thought: Critical thinking requires effort and intellectual labor. For bots, the laziness of accepting pre-packaged ideas and narratives is far easier than the discomfort of curiosity or independent research. The ability to think critically or question the world is lost, not through lack of potential but disinterest.

Example: When faced with complex issues like climate change or economic inequality, bots will often fall back on the most straightforward, digestible narratives, ignoring the nuances of the situation. This intellectual laziness prevents them from engaging deeply with the world around them.

The Robotic Nature of Bots

The term "bot" was chosen because it conveys not only individuals' mental laziness and ignorance but also their robotic, automated nature. Bots don't just parrot information; they often fail to reflect on their behaviors, desires, or beliefs. They move through life on autopilot, responding to stimuli in predictable, unchanging ways without considering their actions' deeper meanings or implications.

Behavioral Repetition Without Reflection

Just as a bot follows its programming, these individuals exhibit repetitive behaviors without reflection. Like their thoughts, their actions are often dictated by social norms and media, rather than internal desires or values. This robotic behavior is most evident in how they react to trends, popular opinions, and societal pressures.

Predictability and Lack of Originality: Bots' responses are predictable because they are driven by external inputs rather than internal reflection. Whether it's their consumer habits, social media interactions, or even their moral stances, bots consistently follow patterns laid out by society, responding in uniform ways that leave little room for innovation or individuality.

Lack of Self-Awareness: One of the critical characteristics of bots is that they are unaware of their behavior. Just as a robot doesn't question its programming, bots rarely question their beliefs or behaviors. They lack self-awareness and the ability to reflect on whether their actions align with their actual values or desires.

Example: During a social movement, bots will often adopt the symbols, language, and slogans of the movement without fully understanding the cause. Their participation is more about conformity than conviction, reflecting the robotic nature of their behavior.

Mimicking Without Understanding

Bots mimic what they see and hear, much like robots following commands. They repeat what they see on TV, what they hear in popular discourse, or what their peers do without truly understanding its meaning. This shallow engagement with the world strips away their individuality and leaves them acting out of habit rather than conviction.

Superficial Engagement: Bots engage with ideas and trends at a surface level. Whether adopting a political stance, following a celebrity or supporting a cause, their participation is often superficial. They mimic the behavior of others, but their understanding is shallow and uncritical.

External Validation: Bots are driven by external validation. They look to the media, celebrities, or societal norms to tell them what is right, what to think, and how to behave. They are not concerned with internal validation or self-awareness because the approval of others dictates their actions.

Example: A bot might adopt a fashion trend simply because it is popular on social media, without considering whether it reflects their style or values. Their behavior is driven by external inputs rather than internal preferences or beliefs.

The Contrast: Non-Bots and the Challenge of Non-Conformity

Non-bots represent the opposite of this robotic behavior. They think critically, act independently, and seek truth, even when uncomfortable. Their willingness to challenge societal norms, question authority, and pursue their path sets them apart from bots. However, this non-conformity often makes them targets of society.

Non-Bots as Outsiders

Because non-bots choose to live authentically, they often find themselves at odds with the majority. Their refusal to conform to bot-like behaviors—whether in thought, action, or belief—makes them stand out. Non-bots prioritize mental, spiritual, and physical freedom over societal acceptance, and as a result, they are often viewed as rebels or misfits.

Victims of Society: Non-bots are frequently victimized by society because they do not fit in with the mainstream. Their independent thinking and rejection of superficial norms can lead to social isolation, ridicule, or even hostility from bots who see them as a threat to the status quo.

The Cost of Independence: Living as a non-bot comes at a cost. Non-bots are willing to bear this cost because they value mental, spiritual, and physical freedom over the convenience of conformity. This choice often puts them in opposition to societal expectations, but it is a sacrifice they are willing to make to live authentically.

Example: A non-bot who questions popular political narratives or refuses to follow superficial trends may be ostracized in social settings. Their refusal to conform makes them a target of criticism or exclusion, but they continue to live in alignment with their values despite the cost.

The Freedom of the Non-Bot

While bots are trapped in cycles of ignorance, repetition, and superficiality, non-bots experience a different kind of freedom. Non-bots are free to explore their beliefs, develop their understanding of the world, and act in ways that align with their values. This mental and spiritual freedom is a crucial distinction between bots and non-bots.

Curiosity and Critical Thinking: Non-bots are driven by curiosity and a desire to understand the world more deeply. They are not content to accept surface-level explanations or conform to societal norms. Instead, they seek to challenge, explore, and grow, even when it leads them to uncomfortable truths.

Living Authentically: Non-bots prioritize authenticity over conformity. While bots follow external validation, non-bots live according to their principles and values. This internal guidance allows them to remain true to themselves, even when faced with societal pressures to conform.

Example: A non-bot may choose a career path that aligns with their passions and values, even if it doesn't come with the social prestige or financial rewards that society values. Their decision is based on personal fulfillment rather than external approval.

Conclusion: The Power of the Term "Bot"

The term "bot" was chosen because it encapsulates the behavior of those who have relinquished their ability to think critically, engage with the world authentically, and pursue truth with curiosity and reflection. Like automated machines, bots operate on external programming—they mimic, repeat, and conform to what society, media, and their surroundings dictate rather than acting from a place of individuality and understanding. Their ignorance, whether intentional or not, results in uniform, unthinking responses that make them resemble programmed robots rather than self-aware individuals.

However, the contrast between bots and non-bots illustrates a fundamental truth about human nature. Non-bots resist the pressures of conformity by choosing a path of critical thinking, curiosity, and authenticity. Though they often face social exclusion or hostility, non-bots remain free—mentally, spiritually, and physically—because they refuse to sacrifice their individuality for the sake of fitting in. Their independence and commitment to truth set them apart from bots, who are content to follow without questioning.

The term "bot" is descriptive and warns about the dangers of ignorance and mindless conformity. In a world where societal pressures can easily erase individuality, the non-bot's journey of self-awareness, critical thinking, and resistance to superficiality becomes all the more valuable. It is a reminder that to live genuinely; one must embrace the discomfort of questioning, thinking, and seeking truth rather than merely existing as a cog in the machine of conformity.

By living as a non-bot, one embarks on a journey of freedom and self-discovery, opposing the robotic uniformity that threatens to consume modern society. Therefore, the term "bot" serves as a powerful metaphor for those who have lost touch with their true selves and as a call to action for those who seek to live with purpose, curiosity, and integrity.

Thank You Thank You to Those Who Relate and Understand

Finding others who relate to and understand the experiences described in this book is reassuring and empowering in a world increasingly defined by polarized views, societal division, and complex interactions. This chapter is a heartfelt expression of gratitude to those who have walked similar paths, faced comparable challenges, and engaged in the ongoing dialogue about navigating a divided world filled with "bots" and the spiritually blind. Your shared insights, resilience, and contributions are invaluable in fostering a deeper understanding of these issues.

Acknowledging Shared Experiences

To those connected with the scenarios and strategies outlined in this book, your shared experiences are a source of solidarity. The frustration of interacting with individuals who adhere to false beliefs, the delicate balance of blending in while staying true to oneself, and the effort required to maintain authenticity in a fragmented society are challenges many of us face. Your willingness to reflect on these experiences is commendable, and your unique perspectives add richness to the collective understanding of these issues.

Navigating Difficult Interactions

Whether in family gatherings, workplaces, or broader social settings, the challenge of engaging with bots can feel isolating. Those who relate to these experiences understand the emotional toll it takes to remain composed while surrounded by uncritical thinking and conformity. Yet, your ability to reflect on these challenges, share your insights, and adapt your approaches is a testament to the strength and depth of your character.

The Shared Frustration: Engaging with those deeply entrenched in false narratives can be exhausting. Yet, you continue to seek ways to foster understanding, showing empathy even in the face of resistance.

The Strength of Connection: Your experiences connect you with a community of others who seek truth and value authenticity, and this shared understanding helps make navigating a bot-filled world more bearable.

Example: A reader reflects on the workplace challenges where they constantly encounter bots entrenched in rigid groupthink. Through shared strategies of deflection and adaptation, they find solace in the knowledge that others, too, are learning to navigate these environments while holding onto their true selves.

Recognizing Your Resilience

Your resilience in maintaining your core beliefs while navigating complex interactions is remarkable. Each of you has shown immense strength in staying authentic in an environment that often rewards conformity. The ability to remain calm, composed, and adaptive without losing your sense of identity reflects a level of emotional intelligence and maturity that deserves recognition.

Emotional and Mental Endurance

The emotional toll of these experiences can weigh heavily, but your ability to rise above the frustration and manage these emotions speaks to your resilience. It is no small feat to continually engage in dialogue with those who may reject your values, yet you persist in seeking meaningful conversations.

Adaptation Without Compromise: You've mastered adapting to environments and social pressures without compromising your core principles.

This balance is critical to maintaining emotional and mental health in a bot-filled world.

Managing Frustration: Many of you have found ways to cope with the inevitable frustration that arises from engaging with individuals who refuse to see or hear the truth. This chapter acknowledges your perseverance and celebrates your emotional endurance.

Example: A reader shares their experience dealing with a close family member whose beliefs are shaped entirely by misinformation. Despite many attempts to challenge these views, they have learned to manage their frustration and focus on maintaining a healthy relationship through empathy and careful adaptation.

Celebrating the Effort to Bridge Divides

One of the most significant challenges in today's world is bridging the divides between people with opposing worldviews. Those of you who have taken on this challenge deserve immense respect. Whether you've chosen to engage in difficult conversations, seek out diverse perspectives, or support others in similar situations, your efforts contribute to a more empathetic and understanding society.

The Courage to Engage

Engaging with individuals whose views starkly oppose your own takes courage, especially when most people avoid such conversations altogether. Your willingness to enter these problematic discussions, equipped with patience and empathy, demonstrates a solid commitment to fostering understanding and mutual respect.

Fostering Meaningful Dialogue: By entering into these conversations with the goal of understanding rather than convincing, you create opportunities for real connection and growth. This approach paves the way for more constructive discussions and greater societal cohesion.

Building Bridges, Not Walls: Your efforts to bridge divides, rather than further them, contribute to a culture where open dialogue and critical thinking can flourish. This is a crucial step toward healing the fractures that characterize modern society.

Example: A reader describes how they've taken on the role of mediator in heated discussions at family gatherings, using deflection techniques and redirection to steer conversations toward more constructive and less emotionally charged topics. Their ability to bridge the gap between opposing viewpoints has helped create a more harmonious family dynamic.

Looking Forward: The Journey Continues

As you continue to navigate the complexities of a divided world, your experiences, and insights will play a pivotal role in shaping a more understanding and cohesive society. This book has outlined strategies to help you maintain your authenticity while navigating interactions with bots, and these tools will serve you well as you move forward.

Part of a Larger Movement

Your journey is a significant movement toward greater awareness, truth-seeking, and critical thinking. The principles and strategies discussed throughout this book are not just for surviving the bot-filled world but for thriving within it. As you continue to apply these techniques, you contribute to a collective effort to awaken others and promote a more thoughtful and compassionate society.

An Ongoing Commitment to Truth: Pursuing truth is a lifelong journey. By committing to this path, you will continue to grow, evolve, and inspire others to do the same.

Inspiring Others: Your resilience, courage, and adaptability serve as a beacon for others struggling to maintain their authenticity in a conformist world. By sharing your experiences and insights, you inspire others to question, reflect, and seek truth.

Example: A non-bot reflects on how the strategies in this book have helped them navigate complex interactions and inspired those around them to start questioning societal narratives. Their journey toward greater truth and understanding has become an example for others.

Conclusion: A Heartfelt Thank You

To all those who relate to the experiences in this book, who have faced the challenges of interacting with bots, and who continue to pursue authenticity and truth, thank you. Your willingness to engage, reflect, and adapt to adversity is inspiring. As you continue this journey, know that you are not alone. Together, we can create spaces for constructive dialogue, bridge divides, and foster a more understanding and enlightened world.

The road ahead may not always be easy. Still, with resilience, empathy, and critical thinking, you are well-equipped to continue navigating the complexities of life in a bot-filled world. Your contribution to the more significant movement toward truth and authenticity is invaluable; I am deeply grateful.

www.ingramcontent.com/pod-product-compliance
Lightning Source LLC
Chambersburg PA
CBHW052159220526
45471CB00004B/1740